Francis Frith's
AROUND PLYMOUTH

PHOTOGRAPHIC MEMORIES

Francis Frith's
AROUND PLYMOUTH

◆

Martin Dunning

FRITH
BOOK Co

First published in the United Kingdom in 2000 by
Frith Book Company Ltd

Hardback Edition 2000
ISBN 1-85937-119-1

Paperback Edition 2001
ISBN 1-85937-389-5

Reprinted in Hardback 2001
ISBN 1-85937-119-1

British Library Cataloguing in Publication Data

Francis Frith's Around Plymouth
Martin Dunning

Frith Book Company Ltd
Frith's Barn, Teffont,
Salisbury, Wiltshire SP3 5QP
Tel: +44 (0) 1722 716 376
Email: info@francisfrith.co.uk
www.francisfrith.co.uk

Printed and bound in Great Britain

CONTENTS

◆

FRANCIS FRITH: *Victorian Pioneer*

FRANCIS FRITH, Victorian founder of the world-famous photographic archive, was a complex and multitudinous man. A devout Quaker and a highly successful Victorian businessman, he was both philosophic by nature and pioneering in outlook.

By 1855 Francis Frith had already established a wholesale grocery business in Liverpool, and sold it for the astonishing sum of £200,000, which is the equivalent today of over £15,000,000. Now a multi-millionaire, he was able to indulge his passion for travel. As a child he had pored over travel books written by early explorers, and his fancy and imagination had been stirred by family holidays to the sublime mountain regions of Wales and Scotland. 'What a land of spirit-stirring and enriching scenes and places!' he had written. He was to return to these scenes of grandeur in later years to 'recapture the thousands of vivid and tender memories', but with a different purpose. Now in his thirties, and captivated by the new science of photography, Frith set out on a series of pioneering journeys to the Nile regions that occupied him from 1856 until 1860.

INTRIGUE AND ADVENTURE

He took with him on his travels a specially-designed wicker carriage that acted as both dark-room and sleeping chamber. These far-flung journeys were packed with intrigue and adventure. In his life story, written when he was sixty-three, Frith tells of being held captive by bandits, and of fighting 'an awful midnight battle to the very point of surrender with a deadly pack of hungry, wild dogs'. Sporting flowing Arab costume, Frith arrived at Akaba by camel seventy years before Lawrence, where he encountered 'desert princes and rival sheikhs, blazing with jewel-hilted swords'.

During these extraordinary adventures he was assiduously exploring the desert regions bordering the Nile and patiently recording the antiquities and peoples with his camera. He was the first photographer to venture beyond the sixth cataract. Africa was still the mysterious 'Dark Continent', and Stanley and Livingstone's historic meeting was a decade into the future. The conditions for picture taking confound belief. He laboured for hours in his wicker dark-room in the sweltering heat of the desert, while the volatile chemicals fizzed dangerously in their trays. Often he was forced to work in remote tombs and caves where conditions were cooler. Back in London he exhibited his photographs and was 'rapturously cheered' by members of the Royal Society. His reputation as a photographer was made overnight. An eminent modern historian has likened their impact on the population of the time to that on our own generation of the first photographs taken on the surface of the moon.

VENTURE OF A LIFE-TIME

Characteristically, Frith quickly spotted the opportunity to create a new business as a specialist publisher of photographs. He lived in an era of immense and sometimes violent change. For the poor in the early part of Victoria's reign work was a drudge and the hours long, and people had precious little free time to enjoy themselves.

Most had no transport other than a cart or gig at their disposal, and had not travelled far beyond the boundaries of their own town or village. However, by the 1870s, the railways had threaded their way across the country, and Bank Holidays and half-day Saturdays had been made obligatory by Act of Parliament. All of a sudden the ordinary working man and his family were able to enjoy days out and see a little more of the world.

With characteristic business acumen, Francis Frith foresaw that these new tourists would enjoy having souvenirs to commemorate their days out. In 1860 he married Mary Ann Rosling and set out with the intention of photographing every city, town and village in Britain. For the next thirty years he travelled the country by train and by pony and trap, producing fine photographs of seaside resorts and beauty spots that were keenly bought by millions of Victorians. These prints were painstakingly pasted into family albums and pored over during the dark nights of winter, rekindling precious memories of summer excursions.

THE RISE OF FRITH & CO

Frith's studio was soon supplying retail shops all over the country. To meet the demand he gathered about him a small team of photographers, and published the work of independent artist-photographers of the calibre of Roger Fenton and Francis Bedford. In order to gain some understanding of the scale of Frith's business one only has to look at the catalogue issued by Frith & Co in 1886: it runs to some 670

pages, listing not only many thousands of views of the British Isles but also many photographs of most European countries, and China, Japan, the USA and Canada – note the sample page shown above from the hand-written *Frith & Co* ledgers detailing pictures taken. By 1890 Frith had created the greatest specialist photographic publishing company in the world, with over 2,000 outlets – more than the combined number that Boots and WH Smith have today! The picture on the right shows the *Frith & Co* display board at Ingleton in the Yorkshire Dales. Beautifully constructed with mahogany frame and gilt inserts, it could display up to a dozen local scenes.

POSTCARD BONANZA

The ever-popular holiday postcard we know today took many years to develop. In 1870 the Post Office issued the first plain cards, with a pre-printed stamp on one face. In 1894 they allowed other publishers' cards to be sent through the mail with an attached adhesive halfpenny stamp. Demand grew rapidly, and in 1895 a new size of postcard was permitted called the

court card, but there was little room for illustration. In 1899, a year after Frith's death, a new card measuring 5.5 x 3.5 inches became the standard format, but it was not until 1902 that the divided back came into being, with address and message on one face and a full-size illustration on the other. *Frith & Co* were in the vanguard of postcard development, and Frith's sons Eustace and Cyril continued their father's monumental task, expanding the number of views offered to the public and recording more and more places in Britain, as the coasts and countryside were opened up to mass travel.

Francis Frith died in 1898 at his villa in Cannes, his great project still growing. The archive he created continued in business for another seventy years. By 1970 it contained over a third of a million pictures of 7,000 cities, towns and villages. The massive photographic record Frith has left to us stands as a living monument to a special and very remarkable man.

Frith's Archive: *A Unique Legacy*

FRANCIS FRITH'S legacy to us today is of immense significance and value, for the magnificent archive of evocative photographs he created provides a unique record of change in 7,000 cities, towns and villages throughout Britain over a century and more. Frith and his fellow studio photographers revisited locations many times down the years to update their views, compiling for us an enthralling and colourful pageant of British life and character.

We tend to think of Frith's sepia views of Britain as nostalgic, for most of us use them to conjure up memories of places in our own lives with which we have family associations. It often makes us forget that to Francis Frith they were records of daily life as it was actually being lived in the cities, towns and villages of his day. The Victorian age was one of great and often bewildering change for ordinary people, and though the pictures evoke an impression of slower times, life was as busy and hectic as it is today.

We are fortunate that Frith was a photographer of the people, dedicated to recording the minutiae of everyday life. For it is this sheer wealth of visual data, the painstaking chronicle of changes in dress, transport, street layouts, buildings, housing, engineering and landscape that captivates us so much today. His remarkable images offer us a powerful link with the past and with the lives of our ancestors.

TODAY'S TECHNOLOGY

Computers have now made it possible for Frith's many thousands of images to be accessed almost instantly. In the Frith archive today, each photograph is carefully 'digitised' then stored on a CD Rom. Frith archivists can locate a single photograph amongst thousands within seconds. Views can be catalogued and sorted under a variety of categories of place and content to the immediate benefit of researchers. Inexpensive reference prints can be created for them at the touch of a mouse button, and a wide range of books and other printed materials assembled and published for a wider, more general readership - in the next twelve months over a hundred Frith local history titles will be published! The

See Frith at www.francisfrith.co.uk

day-to-day workings of the archive are very different from how they were in Francis Frith's time: imagine the herculean task of sorting through eleven tons of glass negatives as Frith had to do to locate a particular sequence of pictures! Yet the archive still prides itself on maintaining the same high standards of excellence laid down by Francis Frith, including the painstaking cataloguing and indexing of every view.

It is curious to reflect on how the internet now allows researchers in America and elsewhere greater instant access to the archive than Frith himself ever enjoyed. Many thousands of individual views can be called up on screen within seconds on one of the Frith internet sites, enabling people living continents away to revisit the streets of their ancestral home town, or view places in Britain where they have enjoyed holidays. Many overseas researchers welcome the chance to view special theme selections, such as transport, sports, costume and ancient monuments.

We are certain that Francis Frith would have heartily approved of these modern developments, for he himself was always working at the very limits of Victorian photographic technology.

THE VALUE OF THE ARCHIVE TODAY

Because of the benefits brought by the computer, Frith's images are increasingly studied by social historians, by researchers into genealogy and ancestory, by architects, town planners, and by teachers and schoolchildren involved in local history projects. In addition, the archive offers every one of

us a unique opportunity to examine the places where we and our families have lived and worked down the years. Immensely successful in Frith's own era, the archive is now, a century and more on, entering a new phase of popularity.

THE PAST IN TUNE WITH THE FUTURE

Historians consider the Francis Frith Collection to be of prime national importance. It is the only archive of its kind remaining in private ownership and has been valued at a million pounds. However, this figure is now rapidly increasing as digital technology enables more and more people around the world to enjoy its benefits.

Francis Frith's archive is now housed in an historic timber barn in the beautiful village of Teffont in Wiltshire. Its founder would not recognize the archive office as it is today. In place of the many thousands of dusty boxes containing glass plate negatives and an all-pervading odour of photographic chemicals, there are now ranks of computer screens. He would be amazed to watch his images travelling round the world at unimaginable speeds through network and internet lines.

The archive's future is both bright and exciting. Francis Frith, with his unshakeable belief in making photographs available to the greatest number of people, would undoubtedly approve of what is being done today with his lifetime's work. His photographs, depicting our shared past, are now bringing pleasure and enlightenment to millions around the world a century and more after his death.

AROUND PLYMOUTH – *An Introduction*

DESPITE THE ROLE it has played in many of Britain's great historic moments and periods, Plymouth is a city apart. Although only 200 miles from London - the same distance as, say, Manchester or Liverpool - its location on the far south-west peninsula has given Plymouth an isolation, even today, that other great cities lack. And it is not merely distance that has isolated the city - its site is bounded on all sides by obstacles. To the north are the stern hills of Dartmoor, to the east the River Plym and to the west the Tamar. Early visitors to the peninsula on which the city would eventually grow would have had to wait for the tide at the Ebb Ford, where Marsh Mills roundabout now stands, before they could cross the Plym and put their feet up at the Crabtree Inn, which over the centuries welcomed many a tired and mud-spattered traveller. Those coming from the west had two choices: to travel north to Gunnislake, the lowest bridge on the Tamar and some twenty miles up the river, and thence via Tavistock and Roborough Down, or to take the ferry that ran at Saltash across the strong tides of the Tamar. Even for land travellers, Plymouth was a place governed by the tides.

Plymouth grew from several small settlements, one of the earliest being Mountbatten, at the mouth of the Plym. The site of an Iron Age cemetery, Mountbatten is thought to have been a trading post from as early as 1000 BC, and in Roman times exported cattle, hides and tin - the first indication of the maritime future of the area. Opposite Mountbatten the small fishing village of Sutton grew around the sheltered harbour of Sutton Pool; it eventually became a town when it was granted a market in 1254 by Henry III. By this time, ships loading tin from the rich port of Plympton had started to use Sutton too, and a lively trade was developing. Fish, hides, lead, wool and cloth were exported, while iron, fruit, wine, onions, garlic and wheat were landed.

1295 saw an event that was to point the way for future development when Edward I assembled the fleet at Plymouth for the first time. The port occupies a crucial strategic position guarding the Western Approaches; it was this factor that was to cement Plymouth's importance, and was probably a consideration when Henry VI granted the borough charter in 1439.

If Plymouth's maritime status brought prosperity, it also meant that the port was often in the front line, especially when Spain was involved. Francis Drake, knighted by Elizabeth I for his circumnavigation of the globe in 1577-80, sailed from Plymouth to 'singe the King of Spain's beard' at Cadiz in 1587 and returned to face his sternest test in 1588 - the Spanish Armada. His apparent bravado on insisting that he finish his game of bowls before engaging the mighty Spanish fleet was dictated by the mundane fact that his ships could not sail until the tide had turned, but what is not in doubt is that his courage and seamanship helped carry the day for the English fleet. Drake did not, as is commonly believed, command the fleet - that responsibility fell to Lord Howard.

Years of fighting Catholic Spain probably explain the streak of puritanism that Plymouth showed for the next hundred years. The city welcomed the noncomformist Pilgrim Fathers when the Mayflower put in for repairs and provisions before sailing for the New World in 1620, and during the Civil War it took Cromwell's side. Plymouth was isolated, as Barnstaple, Bideford and Exeter were all captured by the Royalists and Royalist ships blockaded the Sound.

The nine thousand Parliamentarian troops garrisoned at Plymouth held out under siege for two years, winning a famous victory in December 1643 in the battle which raged around Tothill and Freedom Park. Prince Maurice Road and Mount Gould are named after the Royalist and Parliamentarian commanders. Plymouth was eventually relieved in March 1645 when Cromwell and Fairfax met in the city.

Upon the Restoration of the Monarchy, Charles II decided that Plymouth's defences needed strengthening and commissioned the building of the Citadel. One of the finest and largest restoration forts in the country, it boasted upon completion 152 guns, some of which faced the city as a reminder to

Plymothians of their true place in the order of things.

Secretary of the Navy Samuel Pepys, now known for his diaries but also effectively the founder of the Royal Navy as we know it, visited Plymouth with Charles in 1676 to inspect sites for a new Royal Dockyard. Turnchapel, at the mouth of the Plym, was considered, but struggled for the first half of the 18th century. Fishing still thrived, particularly for pilchards, and trade carried on, but Plymouth has never figured near the top of the table as a commercial port because of its isolation and the lack of nearby markets. Bristol and Liverpool made fortunes from the slave trade, and London's demand for commodities ensured

eventually the prize was given to the Tamar. The Tamar's disadvantages - strong tides, a narrow and winding entrance and often contrary winds - also acted in its favour as they gave the river natural defences from attack; work started on what is now Devonport's South Yard in 1691. Another sign of the port's growing stature was the building in 1696 of Winstanley's 120-foot lighthouse on the Eddystone Rocks fourteen miles off the Hoe, the first in a series of four that would culminate in the current lighthouse built by Douglas in 1878.

Investment notwithstanding, Plymouth that her docks were always busy, but Plymouth slumbered on, depressed and waiting for a turn in the tides of history.

War, by now a recurring theme in the fortunes of the city, provided the catalyst. From 1756 a succession of conflicts - the Seven Years' War, the American War of Independence and the Napoleonic Wars - caused an upturn in Plymouth's fortunes. Her isolation was eased in 1758 with the completion of the Great West Road, although it still took twelve hours to reach Exeter. The Royal Naval Hospital in Stonehouse was built in 1758-62, the dockyard bustled, and in 1812 the famous Scots engineer John Rennie began the construction of the Breakwater. A massive undertaking which was not completed until 1841, the Breakwater was a crucial development. Generations of mariners such as Grenville, Howard and Raleigh had complained that the relatively narrow entrances to the Plym and Tamar were dangerous in foul weather; mariners would often run before the storm to anchor in the sheltered waters of Tor Bay. Now, all a gale-battered ship had to do was slip in through the eastern or western entrances and move into the lee of the breakwater, with plenty of sea-room and calm water in which to anchor.

The railways arrived in 1848-9, and at last Plymouth had a rapid connection with the rest of the country. Isambard Kingdom Brunel's magnificent railway bridge over the Tamar, completed shortly before the great man's death in 1859, had more than a mere practical significance - it was a symbol of Plymouth moving with the times.

John Foulston's Theatre Royal provided entertainment for those who could afford it, while those of lesser means could promenade on the pier or take the air on the Hoe. In the 1920s and 1930s, transatlantic liners anchored in the Sound, discharging passengers such as Charlie Chaplin, Mary Pickford and Rudolph Valentino to catch their train for London from Millbay Docks.

Plymouth prospered, but the clouds of war were gathering again; during the Second World War the city lived through its darkest hours. As a major naval port, Plymouth was high on the Luftwaffe's target list. A series of intense air raids in 1941 left the city devastated; much of the city centre was reduced to rubble, and fine buildings such as the Theatre Royal, the Royal Hotel, the Post Office and the Municipal Buildings were lost for ever. But the people of Plymouth were unbowed. Thousands left the city each night for the foothills of Dartmoor and safety from the bombs, and returned to work the next day. The shell of St Andrew's Church was planted with flowers and hundreds came to worship in the 'Garden Church', while on hot summer evenings, thousands would come from the ruined city to dance on the Hoe with dignitaries like Lady Nancy Astor MP and cock a defiant snook at Nazism.

Once the war was over, thoughts turned to reconstruction. It is a local joke that what Hitler started, the town planners finished: it is true that the new, geometric street plan of the city centre is a little uninspiring, but St Andrew's still stands, and the broad sweep of Armada Way leads one seawards to the heights of the Hoe.

Stand on the Promenade on a clear day and turn through 360°, and all around are reminders of Plymouth's past. To the north are the blue hills of Dartmoor, source of the tin that caused the port to come into existence. West is the entrance to the Tamar, home to the frigates, aircraft carriers and submarines which slip in and out of port in all weathers, even in peacetime. Merchantmen anchor in the lee of the Breakwater, ready to discharge their cargoes of petrol and fertiliser on the wharves of the Plym, and trawlers set sail from a largely unchanged Barbican for the fishing grounds. And on the horizon, the Eddystone light winks unceasingly, a beacon for mariners heading for one of Britain's great ports.

THE HOE 1890 22471

Taken from Devil's Point looking across Firestone bay with the Hoe just visible on the far right. The large colonnaded building is the Winter Villa, built by the Earl of Mount Edgecumbe for his wife, who found the winters at Mount Edgecumbe House a little too draughty.

VIEW FROM THE HOE c1876 8349

Taken from the site of the old Hoe Police Station and lock-up before the pier was built, this view shows a largely undeveloped West Hoe (the grassy area at centre). The large block of houses on the point at centre left still stands and is now mostly hotels.

THE ESPLANADE AND HOE 1889 22363

One hundred feet above sea level, and with commanding views of the Sound and the English Channel, the Hoe is where Sir Francis Drake is reputed to have played his famous game of bowls while waiting for the Armada to arrive in 1588.

THE HOE AND PIER 1889 22368

The prominent structure on the top of Staddon Heights (just right of centre) is not, as local myth says, a windbreak for the golf course on the top of the Heights; it was actually constructed as a gunnery range for troops stationed at Bovisand Fort, on the headland below.

THE ESPLANADE HOE 1889 22361
The fine colonnaded building second from left is the
Grand Hotel; it still stands, as does Eliot Terrace to its right.
3 Eliot Terrace was the home of Lord and Lady Astor for
many years. Nancy Astor was the first woman MP in the
country, representing Plymouth Sutton from 1919–46.

THE PIER FROM SMEATON TOWER 1889 22372

In the middle distance to the right are ships anchored in the Hamoaze, which turns north up the Tamar to Devonport Dockyard. The narrow entrance to the Hamoaze (hidden at centre) is easily guarded but, in times of sail, presented difficulties for the fleet if it needed to sail in a hurry and on a foul tide.

THE PIER FROM BELOW 1889 22375

The building next to the Grand Hotel, a victim of the Luftwaffe in the blitz, became the home of the Royal Western Yacht Club in 1880. The club subsequently moved to West Hoe and, in the 1980s, to Queen Anne's Battery. The doors above the steps on the right were for many years used by the Leander Swimming Club.

SMEATON TOWER 1890 22365

This lighthouse once occupied the feared Eddystone Rock, 14 miles south of the Hoe. Built by John Smeaton, it was the third lighthouse on the rock; it shone from 1756 to 1890, when the present lighthouse, designed by Douglas, was completed.

MOUNT EDGECUMBE 1889 22385

The wooded estate of Mount Edgecumbe is the hereditary seat of the Earls of Mount Edgecumbe. The clearing in the centre is the site of the famous folly, while on the right the top of Mount Edgecumbe House can be seen peeping from the trees.

THE PIER 1889 22377

Plymouth's pier was destroyed in the blitz It was built in 1884, extending out from the old Bull Ring, a popular spot for political meetings, particularly in the last century during the noisy campaign that led in 1832 to Plymouth becoming three constituencies and Stonehouse and Devonport having their own MPs for the first time.

THE HOE AND PIER 1890 27530

The centre of the Pier, now covered, was a popular venue for concert parties, boxing, wrestling, roller skating and tea dances. To take the sea air in the company of other fashionable Victorians, one entered through the turnstiles on each side of the clock for the princely sum of 2d.

VIEW FROM THE PIER 1892 30590

The building high up on the left houses the Plymouth Laboratory of the Marine Biological Association of Great Britain, now one of the world's leading marine research organisations. The building also housed the aquarium before the opening of the national marine aquarium on the Barbican in 1998. Right of the MBA is the Citadel, the city's biggest fortress.

THE PIER 1892
The steps and diving board below the Sunlight Soap advertisement belonged to the Plymouth Ladies Swimming Club. One ex-member recalls completing the two-mile swim from the Breakwater in 1927 in 58 minutes and two thirds of a second. Her sister held the record of 48 minutes.

◆

VIEW FROM THE PIER 1892
The rocks in the centre are where Tinside Pool now stands. Further back, to the right of the triangular buttress, is the site of the Royal Plymouth Corinthian Yacht Club and beyond that, the Cattewater.

THE PIER 1892 30585

VIEW FROM THE PIER 1892 30591

THE PIER AND DRAKE'S ISLAND 1892 30583

Drake's Island was originally known as St Nicholas Island; it was owned by the Priors of Plympton, who used it as a rabbit warren. It was fortified in 1549 and the defences were later extended by Plymouth's favourite son - hence the name change.

VIEW FROM STADDON 1889 22383

The Mountbatten peninsula (foreground) guards and shelters the Cattewater and Sutton Pool (right). Occupied since prehistoric times, ownership was returned to the city in 1995 after nearly 70 years of occupation by the RAF. In the 1920s the personnel list included one Aircraftman Shaw - Lawrence of Arabia.

THE PIER 1898 41930
The five square miles of Plymouth Sound provide a
fine safe anchorage. Jennycliff Bay (in the middle distance on the left) is as popular a spot now as in 1898,
especially if the wind is in the east and the great bulk
of Staddon Heights acts as a natural windbreak.

VIEW FROM SMEATON POINT 1898 41929
The curious octagonal building in the foreground was once the Hoe Police Station and was also a camera obscura. The building by the little harbour was for many years the home of the Royal Western Yacht Club and is now the Waterfront Restaurant.

THE BREAKWATER 1893 31954
The completion of the Breakwater in 1844 after 32 years' work secured Plymouth's standing as a major port. Designed by John Rennie, and utilising 3,500,000 tons of limestone from quarries at Oreston, its construction meant that for the first time ships did not have to use the Plym or the Tamar to anchor in a storm.

THE HOE 1902 48781

The Bandstand (foreground) once stood on the site of today's public bowling green before moving to this site near Smeaton's Tower. Regular performers included the Royal Marine Band; the Bandstand was hit during the blitz and subsequently pulled down.

THE PIER 1898 41931

The paddle steamers ran trips to the River Yealm and as far west as Looe. In a curious echo of history, many of today's tourist boats leave from the site of the old pier for similar destinations, and also for cruises up the Tamar.

THE HOE 1904 52403
The area covered by trees below the octagonal Police Station
was for a long time home to the Mallard Café; it is now the
site of the Dome, one of Plymouth's major attractions.

THE HOE 1904 52398

The prominent building in the centre was used for many years as a nursery by the city parks department. The exposed position of the bandstand meant that it had to have a revolving glass screen to prevent the performers' music blowing away!

THE BANDSTAND 1902 48782

In the middle distance on the left are the masts of ships in Millbay Docks. In the 1920s Millbay Docks were busy with passengers being ferried from the railway out to liners such as the Queen Mary and Normandie.

THE PIER 1913 65981

Modern excursion boats are diesel rather than steam, and have propellers instead of paddle wheels. Paddlers lasted longer than is generally known, however: the dockyard was using paddle tugs until the mid 1980s.

THE HOE, SMEATON TOWER AND BANDSTAND 1913 65980

The stone pavilion on the left, known to Plymothians as the 'Wedding Cake', was built in 1891-2 when Alderman Harris was Mayor. The garden directly below it is now a garden of remembrance to the dead of Dunkirk, Normandy, Korea, Malaysia and other campaigns.

SMEATON'S TOWER AND THE BANDSTAND 1913 65979
As well as being used for promenading, the Hoe has
always been the vantage point from which Plymothians
have watched the arrivals and departures of vessels,
from Sir Francis Chichester's 'Gypsy Moth IV' to the
battle-weary ships of the Falklands war.

THE PIER 1924 75896
The Pier not only acted as a magnet for tourists but
also for local traders, who would set up their carts,
wagons and stalls near the entrance hoping to catch
some trade from alighting tram passengers.

THE PIER AND DRAKE'S ISLAND 1924 75899

On his return from his circumnavigation in 1580, Drake anchored in the lee of the island while he sent messengers ashore to check if Queen Elizabeth was still alive and, if so, whether he was still in favour. He managed to ensure the latter by sending several tons of stolen Spanish gold to London.

THE NAVAL AND ARMADA MEMORIALS 1924 75908

In 1888 the Hoe became a park and the Armada Memorial (left) was erected to mark the tercentenary of Drake's great victory. The Naval Memorial was extended considerably after World War Two.

THE LIDO AND WALKS 1934 86216

The magnificent art deco Tinside Lido and Swimming Pool, completed in 1933, was a popular venue for generations of Plymouth children, mainly during the summer holidays, as the salt-water pool had no heating. More sedentary pleasures could be had by hiring a chalet, the roofs of some of which can be seen in the left foreground.

DRAKE'S STATUE 1930 83293

The Café on the left was one of Hitler's victims; it was replaced by a vast Nissen Hut, which served teas well into the 1980s. Visible just behind Drake's Statue is the corner of the bowling green. The terrace behind is also gone; the Register Office now stands on the site.

FROM THE CITADEL 1904 52400

On the far right, the building with the conservatory and tower is the old Hoegate School. The fine avenue of elm trees on the left suffered greatly from the ravages of Dutch Elm Disease in the 1970s.

THE ROYAL CITADEL GATE 1924 75921

Construction of the Citadel commenced in 1670 on the orders of Charles II. It is now home to 29 Commando Regiment Royal Artillery; it was considerably extended in the 1980s. Just visible through the gate are some of the magnificent Restoration buildings that surround the parade ground.

THE SOUTH AFRICAN MEMORIAL 1904 52404
Only a year old when this picture was taken, this pink granite obelisk was erected in memory of Christian Victor,
Prince of Schleswig Holstein and grandson of Queen Victoria, who died in the Boer War. It also serves as a memorial to the men of the Gloucestershire, Somerset and Devonshire regiments who died in the same campaign. A chip
on the south west corner is shrapnel damage from the blitz.

THE SOUTH AFRICAN MONUMENT AND GUILDHALL 1904 52399

This view shows the commanding field of fire available to gunners on the Citadel, from where this picture was taken. Plymouth was staunchly parliamentarian during the Civil War; when Charles II built the Citadel, the fact that there were gun emplacements facing inland would not have gone unnoticed by the local population.

THE BARBICAN 1890 22474

Built around Sutton Pool, site of one of the original settlements in the area, the Barbican is home to Plymouth's fishing fleet. The cobbled streets and granite steps remain unchanged, but in place of shipping offices and fish salesmen are now ice cream parlours, cafés and souvenir shops.

SUTTON POOL 1904 52413A

Declining stocks and fish quotas have taken their toll of the fleet, and Sutton Pool now has far fewer boats. The building on the right is the old Barbican Police Station, now used by Cap'n Jasper's burger bar, and the quay has been extended slightly so that the mooring bollards now sprout from the pavement!

ONION SELLERS 1907 59208

The onions on the shoulders of these two boys, photographed at the Mayflower Steps, may well have been French. Breton onion sellers were once a common sight on the streets of Plymouth.

THE BARBICAN c1955 P60050
The open building on the left, now occupied by Dartington Glass, was until the 1990s the old fish market, built in 1892. The warehouses in the background have been converted into flats, and the area of Sutton Pool on the far right is now a marina.

THE BARBICAN c1955 P60069
The white painted steps, centre left, are the Mayflower Steps, scene of the Pilgrim Fathers' departure for the New World in 1620. On the right, the coal wharf is now home to the new fish market and National Marine Aquarium, and the harbour now has lock gates to prevent it drying out at low tide.

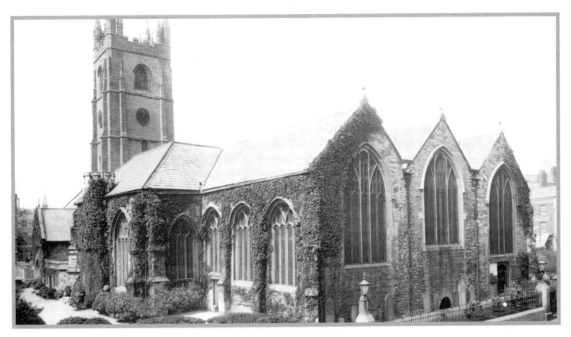

St Andrew's Church 1889 22399

St Andrew's is the mother church of Plymouth; there is evidence that a Christian community used the site as early as the 8th century. Construction of the present building commenced in 1370. The church was burned down in the blitz, but restoration started in 1949 and the church was finally reconsecrated in 1957.

St Andrew's Cross 1900 45862

After St Andrew's had been reduced to a shell by the Luftwaffe in 1941, somebody put a wooden board above the door with the word Resurgam on it, from the Latin for 'I will rise again'. Ever since then the north door (left) of St Andrew's has been known as the Resurgam door.

THE GUILDHALL 1889 22394

The fine tower at the west end of St Andrew's, built by Thomas Yogge in 1481 and now housing a peal of ten bells, used to look out over Guildhall Square, which is now a car park.

THE GUILDHALL AND POST OFFICE 1889 22388

The Guildhall (left) and Municipal Buildings (right, containing the Lord Mayor's Parlour) were opened in 1874 by the Prince of Wales, who later became Edward VII. They were both gutted by fire on the night of 3 March 1941.

St Andrew's Cross 1895 36320

Erected in 1895 as a memorial after the removal of an ancient burial ground, St Andrew's Cross was damaged the night before the church went up in flames and was subsequently removed. The only remaining piece is the copper cross from the very top, which is now in the north aisle of St Andrew's.

THE GUILDHALL 1889 22395

Taken from the vicinity of the Boer War memorial, this picture shows how much more ornate the Guildhall was before its destruction and subsequent rebuilding. The spire on the ridge of the main roof no longer exists, and the tower now has a plain copper roof.

THE GUILDHALL AND POST OFFICE 1904 52408

The main public entrance to the Post Office is just out of sight around the corner on the right. Staff entered through the central doors. Telegraphy equipment was housed on the first floor, and the top floor contained the staff rest-rooms.

THE GUILDHALL 1924 75920
The new stained glass window in the tower of St Andrew's, installed after the war, was designed by John Piper (who also designed the windows in the east end); it commemorates Nancy Astor and her husband, who were Mayor and Mayoress during the war years.

OLD TOWN STREET 1889 22398
The modern Old Town Street runs more or less on the path of the old one. The spot where the carriage is driving is now on the pavement to the west of the Roundabout at St Andrew's Cross and on the south side of Royal Parade.

BEDFORD STREET 1904 52407
The imposing Prudential Building (centre) was damaged during the war, but still stood in 1945.
It was demolished in 1947 to make way for the new street plan. Its tower occupied a position which
today is on the west side of Armada Way near where the Western Morning News office now stands.

BEDFORD STREET 1913 65976

This scene shows some well-known Plymouth business-es. Dingles (far left) are still in the town, although these days owned by House of Fraser, and Underwoods were well-known grocers. John Yeo, along with Spooners (out of sight at the end of the street) was eventually taken over by Debenhams.

THE GUILDHALL AND BEDFORD STREET 1904 52409
The Bedford Hotel later became Bateman's Opticians, with a giant pair of spectacles that many local people still remember. The northern end of the Post Office (just visible down Basket Street in the centre) would now be on Royal Parade outside Dingles.

BEDFORD STREET 1913 65975
Here we see more well-known Plymouth names. Many Plymothians remember buying school bags and suitcases from Webb and Son, who dealt in leather goods. Goodbody's Café was a popular spot, and indeed there is still a pub of that name on Mutley Plain.

OLD TOWN STREET c1960 P60085

After the war, the remains of the city centre were demolished to make way for a new, more regular street plan. In this picture the new Post Office is still under construction on the right.

ROYAL PARADE c1960 P60101

This photograph was taken from roughly the site of the old Post Office. The bus on the other side of Royal Parade behind the scooter is one of the first to have the door at the front and no conductor.

DRAKE'S CIRCUS c1955
The Guinness clock at the top of Old Town Street was a popular rendezvous. It stood where the southern end of Drake's Circus shopping centre now stands. The corner this side of the obvious awnings is now home to Burton's.

COBOURG STREET c1955
The north side of Cobourg Street is almost unchanged. The Public Secondary School (right), whose most well-known old girl is Angela Rippon, is now part of the University of Plymouth, and the playground is occupied by satellite dishes.

DRAKE'S CIRCUS c1955   P60032

COBOURG STREET c1955   P60038

POUND STREET c1955 P60051

To the right of the junction at the far end of Pound Street is the Harvest Home, a much-loved pub which was demolished in 1964. The tall building beyond the Harvest Home still stands; it is home to hairdressers Maison Terry and a number of cafés.

THE MUSEUM AND FREE LIBRARY 1892 30581A

Although bombed during the war, the museum, art gallery and library are still at the bottom of Tavistock Road. Just out of the picture on the left was the surgery of the school dentist - something pointed out by almost every Plymothian over fifty to see this picture!

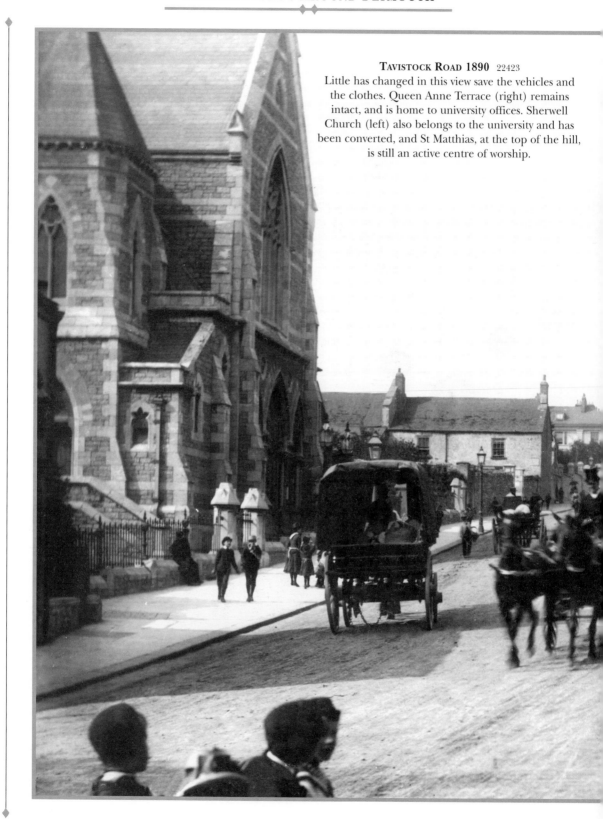

TAVISTOCK ROAD 1890 22423
Little has changed in this view save the vehicles and the clothes. Queen Anne Terrace (right) remains intact, and is home to university offices. Sherwell Church (left) also belongs to the university and has been converted, and St Matthias, at the top of the hill, is still an active centre of worship.

MUTLEY PLAIN 1904 52412

The private houses on the left are now occupied by pizza take-aways and newsagents. The Co-op is still on the same premises, albeit with a new frontage, and Mutley Baptist Church (left) remains unchanged. The house on the corner of Alexandra Road (right) was for many years a dentist's.

MUTLEY PLAIN 1904 52413

Take away the trees, update the shop frontages and turn the road into a dual carriageway, and you see Mutley as it is today, except that the Hyde Park Hotel (from where this view was taken) is now on an island and Mutley Methodist (left) has been pulled down.

THE CATHOLIC CATHEDRAL 1889

The Cathedral Church of St Margaret Mary, with its elegant slim spire, was started in 1856 by Bishop Vaughan. Next to it in this picture stands Notre Dame High School, run by nuns who lived in the convent attached to the school. The site is now occupied by sheltered housing.

◆

GEORGE STREET 1889

The imposing columns are the entrance to the Theatre Royal, which stood on the site now occupied by the ABC Cinema. Theatregoers used to be able to hire a boy from the Barbican to queue for them, a service which cost the princely sum of 6d in the 1930s.

THE CATHOLIC CATHEDRAL 1889   22409

GEORGE STREET 1889   22397

THE CLOCK TOWER 1892 30597
Cousins' Hotel (left) and Genoni's, next to it, were popular refreshment stops for actors and stage crew between rehearsals. That function for the modern Theatre Royal (built roughly on the site of the GWR offices) is fulfilled by The Bank, which in this picture (behind the columns) is still a bank.

THE THEATRE ROYAL AND DERRY'S CLOCK 1907 59204
Derry's Clock, erected in 1862 by Samuel Derry, was known to generations of Plymothians as 'the four-faced deceiver' because all the clock faces told slightly different times. The clock still stands behind the new Theatre Royal.

THE CLOCK TOWER 1924 75922

Derry's Clock had four drinking fountains at its base with cups (long since gone) that hung on chains. The underground toilets on the right reputedly had their 'Ladies' and 'Gents' signs swapped round by Lawrence of Arabia when he was stationed in Plymouth.

UNION STREET 1889 22359

A surprising amount of this part of Union Street still exists. The corner on the left is now taxi offices and the adjoining buildings are night clubs and shops. The projecting building at centre left is the Clipper pub. The Octagon (centre) was in 1890 private homes rather than burger, pizza and kebab houses.

UNION STREET 1904 52406
This view, taken in the direction of Stonehouse, shows
some high street names that are still in business today.
Stead and Simpson's and Oliver's now sell their shoes
in New George Street. Local lore has it that
respectable ladies stuck to one side of the street,
'working girls' to the other, to avoid confusion.

DEVONPORT, HALFPENNY BRIDGE 1904 52427
Upstream of Halfpenny Bridge, Stonehouse creek used to run as far as Pennycomequick, but was progressively filled over the years. Downstream (right) from the bridge is the Cremyll Ferry and Royal Willam Yard. The toll-house was the white building on the left; the toll, as the name suggested, was a halfpenny.

DEVONPORT, ROYAL MARINE BARRACKS 1890 22448
Situated on Durnford Street, which runs parallel to Stonehouse Creek, the Royal Marine Barracks were built in 1867 using a mixture of Plymouth limestone and granite from the moors and originally housed 1400 men.

DEVONPORT, MOUNT WISE 1890 22468
A large marina now stands (or rather floats) on this site. The hill on the right has a memorial to Devonport's most famous son, Captain Scott, and on the riverside in the middle distance the large barn-like building is King Billy Yard, the oldest covered shipyard still standing in Europe.

DEVONPORT
Boer Gun 1904
Inscribed 'Ready Aye Ready', this captured Boer gun is a memorial to Royal Marines and sailors from HMS 'Doris'. Fittingly, it stands high on a hill overlooking the dockyard from which HMS 'Doris' would have sailed to South Africa.

DEVONPORT
HMS 'Lion' and 'Implacable' 1890
These old ships of the line were probably used as training ships for young recruits. Outdated, mothballed or paid-off vessels were often moored at this spot off the mouth of Millbrook Lake. The much-loved aircraft carrier 'Ark Royal' spent some years here prior to being towed away for scrap in 1979.

DEVONPORT, BOER GUN 1904 52415A

DEVONPORT, HMS 'LION' AND 'IMPLACABLE' 1890 22467

DEVONPORT, TORPOINT FERRY BRIDGE 1890 22462

Ferries crossed at this point since the 18th century, carrying not only people, carriages and goods but, from 1800, the post for the Truro coach. 'Jemima', built at Stonehouse, became the first steam ferry in service in 1826, but was quickly replaced by steam driven chain ferries.

TORPOINT, THE FERRY 1925 78415

The earliest ferries were little more than two hulls with a platform suspended between them, and the crossing could take some time owing to the strong tides that run in the Tamar. Modern chain ferries, little affected by the tides, rattle and clank their way across in about ten minutes.

TORPOINT, THE FERRY c1955 T63003
The lorry at the head of the ferry queue is probably taking empties back to the Plymouth Brewery near Halfpenny Bridge in Stonehouse. Fondly remembered by older drinkers, Plymouth Brewery was eventually taken over by Courage; after that, the beer never tasted quite the same.

TORPOINT
The Ferry c1955
The steep loading ramp of the ferries caused problems for longer vehicles, which were in danger of grounding. The brown and cream Co-op coaches had a bevel taken off the rear bodywork to prevent this happening.

TORPOINT
The Ferry c1955
At one time cars were fitted so tightly onto the ferries that it was impossible to open the doors. The obvious dangers of this in case of fire or sinking caused a public outcry, and eventually the ferries were widened.

TORPOINT, THE FERRY c1955 T63004

TORPOINT, THE FERRY c1955 T63006

TORPOINT, FORE STREET c1955 T63014

On the left is Wheeler's Hotel, and at the top of the street, just visible, is the hop leaf symbol of Simond's Brewery - once a common sight on local pubs. On the right are two trade names that are rarely seen today - Woodbines and Capstan Full Strength.

TORPOINT, FORE STREET AND FERRY QUEUE c1955 T63015

The ferry queue no longer blocks Fore Street - it takes the road on the right down to a large waiting area by the river. The three men in white hats are probably 'Tiffies' - Artificers from the training establishment at HMS 'Fisgard', now closed.

SALTASH, ROYAL ALBERT BRIDGE 1890 22477

The rich fields of the Tamar Valley have long been the source of Plymouth's fruit and vegetables. Tamar barges such as the one in the centre of this picture would bring produce down from Calstock, Gunnislake and Bere Alston and land them at Cornwall Street in Devonport.

SALTASH, THE ROYAL ALBERT BRIDGE 1890 22480

The Royal Albert Bridge, completed in 1859, is a fitting memorial to the great Victorian engineer Isambard Kingdom Brunel. The Admiralty stipulated that it must be at least 100 feet above the water to allow the passage of ships.

SALTASH, THE FERRY 1924 76023

The earliest record of a ferry here dates from 1337. In 1832 a consortium led by the Earl of Morley established the first steam ferry. The vessel in this picture came to a sad end - it was sunk off Portreath while being towed to Wales after being sold.

SALTASH, THE TAMAR BRIDGE c1965 S50091

The completion of the road bridge in 1961 signalled the end of the Saltash Ferry. The bridge and the Torpoint Ferry are managed by a joint committee, with revenues from the bridge subsidising the maintenance and running of the ferry.

PLYMPTON, ST MARY'S 1890 22512

On the right of the photograph in front of the church is the old priory. The monks had their own path through the woods to the church, where they had their own pews. Behind the church, hidden in the trees, is Plympton station, which closed in 1959, and in the centre of the picture is the old St Mary's Church of England School.

PLYMPTON, THE TOWN HALL 1890 22515

This view remains almost unchanged, save that the horse and cart have been replaced by the motor car. The arched walk under the Town Hall is known as the Butterwalk.

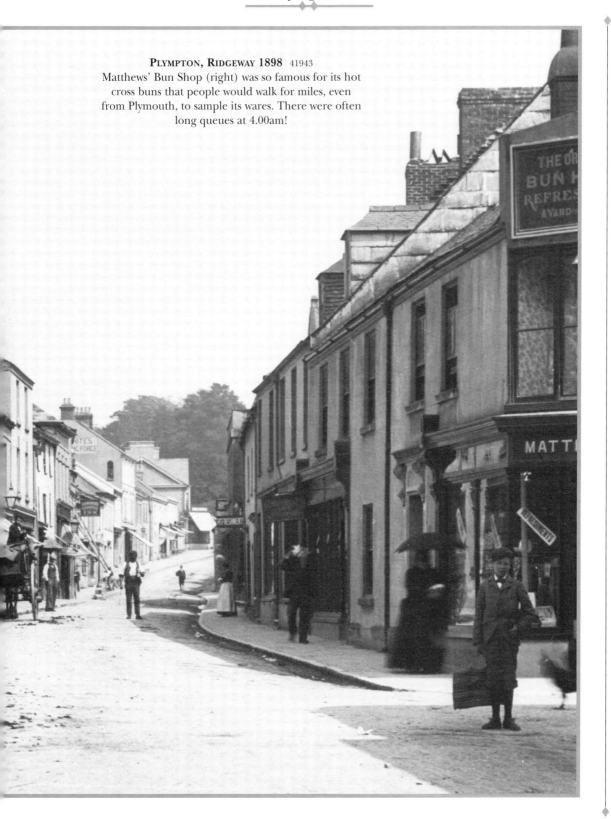

PLYMPTON, RIDGEWAY 1898 41943
Matthews' Bun Shop (right) was so famous for its hot
cross buns that people would walk for miles, even
from Plymouth, to sample its wares. There were often
long queues at 4.00am!

PLYMOUTH, FERRY HOUSE AND PLANTATIONS 1901 46333

The quiet estuary of the River Yealm (pronounced 'Yam') lies to the east of Plymouth. The foot ferry still runs at this spot, summoned by shouting 'over' or by whistling. The villages of Newton Ferrers and Noss Mayo lie just up the river to the left.

BERE FERRERS 1898 42257

Bere Ferrers lies north of Plymouth on the isolated peninsula that divides the estuaries of the Tamar and its tributary the Tavy (right). Bere Ferrers is the first stop on the Tamar Valley railway line which runs up to Gunnislake; it has the distinction of being one of the few lines on which the train sometimes stops to allow passengers to take photographs!

PLYMOUTH, DRAKE'S ISLAND 1890 22426

Now in Cornwall, Mount Edgecumbe, from where this picture was taken, was once part of Devon. The nearby village of Kingsand still has a stone showing where the boundary used to lie. The folly was constructed using stone from the tower of St Lawrence's church, which used to stand on the site now occupied by Royal William Yard in Stonehouse.

PLYMOUTH, DRAKE'S ISLAND FROM MOUNT EDGECUMBE 1890 22427

The broad channel between Drake's Island and Mount Edgecumbe, known as The Bridges, is only navigable via one narrow channel, which is why ships always appear to take 'the long way round', following Drake Passage to the east and north of the Island, as the three-master in this picture is probably doing.

PLYMOUTH, FROM MOUNT EDGECUMBE 1890 22425
In the centre is the Edgecumbes' Winter Villa, which later became the convent and nursing home Nazareth House. It was completely rebuilt after a fire. The grassy area to the left is Devil's Point, a popular picnic and walking spot.

PLYMOUTH, MOUNT EDGECUMBE HOUSE 1890 22436
The building of Mount Edgecumbe House was started by Piers Edgecumbe in 1539 and remodelled in the 17th and 18th centuries. It was badly damaged by German incendiaries in March 1941 and subsequently restored, but the highest tower in this picture was never rebuilt.

Index

Frith Book Co Titles

www.francisfrith.co.uk

The Frith Book Company publishes over 100 new titles each year. A selection of those currently available are listed below. For latest catalogue please contact Frith Book Co.

Town Books 96 pages, approx 100 photos. County and Themed Books 128 pages, approx 150 photos (unless specified). All titles hardback laminated case and jacket except those indicated pb (paperback)

Amersham, Chesham & Rickmansworth (pb)		
	1-85937-340-2	£9.99
Ancient Monuments & Stone Circles	1-85937-143-4	£17.99
Aylesbury (pb)	1-85937-227-9	£9.99
Bakewell	1-85937-113-2	£12.99
Barnstaple (pb)	1-85937-300-3	£9.99
Bath (pb)	1-85937-419-0	£9.99
Bedford (pb)	1-85937-205-8	£9.99
Berkshire (pb)	1-85937-191-4	£9.99
Berkshire Churches	1-85937-170-1	£17.99
Blackpool (pb)	1-85937-382-8	£9.99
Bognor Regis (pb)	1-85937-431-x	£9.99
Bournemouth	1-85937-067-5	£12.99
Bradford (pb)	1-85937-204-x	£9.99
Brighton & Hove(pb)	1-85937-192-2	£8.99
Bristol (pb)	1-85937-264-3	£9.99
British Life A Century Ago (pb)	1-85937-213-9	£9.99
Buckinghamshire (pb)	1-85937-200-7	£9.99
Camberley (pb)	1-85937-222-8	£9.99
Cambridge (pb)	1-85937-422-0	£9.99
Cambridgeshire (pb)	1-85937-420-4	£9.99
Canals & Waterways (pb)	1-85937-291-0	£9.99
Canterbury Cathedral (pb)	1-85937-179-5	£9.99
Cardiff (pb)	1-85937-093-4	£9.99
Carmarthenshire	1-85937-216-3	£14.99
Chelmsford (pb)	1-85937-310-0	£9.99
Cheltenham (pb)	1-85937-095-0	£9.99
Cheshire (pb)	1-85937-271-6	£9.99
Chester	1-85937-090-x	£12.99
Chesterfield	1-85937-378-x	£9.99
Chichester (pb)	1-85937-228-7	£9.99
Colchester (pb)	1-85937-188-4	£8.99
Cornish Coast	1-85937-163-9	£14.99
Cornwall (pb)	1-85937-229-5	£9.99
Cornwall Living Memories	1-85937-248-1	£14.99
Cotswolds (pb)	1-85937-230-9	£9.99
Cotswolds Living Memories	1-85937-255-4	£14.99
County Durham	1-85937-123-x	£14.99
Croydon Living Memories	1-85937-162-0	£9.99
Cumbria	1-85937-101-9	£14.99
Dartmoor	1-85937-145-0	£14.99

Derby (pb)	1-85937-367-4	£9.99
Derbyshire (pb)	1-85937-196-5	£9.99
Devon (pb)	1-85937-297-x	£9.99
Dorset (pb)	1-85937-269-4	£9.99
Dorset Churches	1-85937-172-8	£17.99
Dorset Coast (pb)	1-85937-299-6	£9.99
Dorset Living Memories	1-85937-210-4	£14.99
Down the Severn	1-85937-118-3	£14.99
Down the Thames (pb)	1-85937-278-3	£9.99
Down the Trent	1-85937-311-9	£14.99
Dublin (pb)	1-85937-231-7	£9.99
East Anglia (pb)	1-85937-265-1	£9.99
East London	1-85937-080-2	£14.99
East Sussex	1-85937-130-2	£14.99
Eastbourne	1-85937-061-6	£12.99
Edinburgh (pb)	1-85937-193-0	£8.99
England in the 1880s	1-85937-331-3	£17.99
English Castles (pb)	1-85937-434-4	£9.99
English Country Houses	1-85937-161-2	£17.99
Essex (pb)	1-85937-270-8	£9.99
Exeter	1-85937-126-4	£12.99
Exmoor	1-85937-132-9	£14.99
Falmouth	1-85937-066-7	£12.99
Folkestone (pb)	1-85937-124-8	£9.99
Glasgow (pb)	1-85937-190-6	£9.99
Gloucestershire	1-85937-102-7	£14.99
Great Yarmouth (pb)	1-85937-426-3	£9.99
Greater Manchester (pb)	1-85937-266-x	£9.99
Guildford (pb)	1-85937-410-7	£9.99
Hampshire (pb)	1-85937-279-1	£9.99
Hampshire Churches (pb)	1-85937-207-4	£9.99
Harrogate	1-85937-423-9	£9.99
Hastings & Bexhill (pb)	1-85937-131-0	£9.99
Heart of Lancashire (pb)	1-85937-197-3	£9.99
Helston (pb)	1-85937-214-7	£9.99
Hereford (pb)	1-85937-175-2	£9.99
Herefordshire	1-85937-174-4	£14.99
Hertfordshire (pb)	1-85937-247-3	£9.99
Horsham (pb)	1-85937-432-8	£9.99
Humberside	1-85937-215-5	£14.99
Hythe, Romney Marsh & Ashford	1-85937-256-2	£9.99

Available from your local bookshop or from the publisher

Frith Book Co Titles (continued)

Ipswich (pb)	1-85937-424-7	£9.99	St Ives (pb)	1-85937415-8	£9.99
Ireland (pb)	1-85937-181-7	£9.99	Scotland (pb)	1-85937-182-5	£9.99
Isle of Man (pb)	1-85937-268-6	£9.99	Scottish Castles (pb)	1-85937-323-2	£9.99
Isles of Scilly	1-85937-136-1	£14.99	Sevenoaks & Tunbridge	1-85937-057-8	£12.99
Isle of Wight (pb)	1-85937-429-8	£9.99	Sheffield, South Yorks (pb)	1-85937-267-8	£9.99
Isle of Wight Living Memories	1-85937-304-6	£14.99	Shrewsbury (pb)	1-85937-325-9	£9.99
Kent (pb)	1-85937-189-2	£9.99	Shropshire (pb)	1-85937-326-7	£9.99
Kent Living Memories	1-85937-125-6	£14.99	Somerset	1-85937-153-1	£14.99
Lake District (pb)	1-85937-275-9	£9.99	South Devon Coast	1-85937-107-8	£14.99
Lancaster, Morecambe & Heysham (pb)	1-85937-233-3	£9.99	South Devon Living Memories	1-85937-168-x	£14.99
Leeds (pb)	1-85937-202-3	£9.99	South Hams	1-85937-220-1	£14.99
Leicester	1-85937-073-x	£12.99	Southampton (pb)	1-85937-427-1	£9.99
Leicestershire (pb)	1-85937-185-x	£9.99	Southport (pb)	1-85937-425-5	£9.99
Lincolnshire (pb)	1-85937-433-6	£9.99	Staffordshire	1-85937-047-0	£12.99
Liverpool & Merseyside (pb)	1-85937-234-1	£9.99	Stratford upon Avon	1-85937-098-5	£12.99
London (pb)	1-85937-183-3	£9.99	Suffolk (pb)	1-85937-221-x	£9.99
Ludlow (pb)	1-85937-176-0	£9.99	Suffolk Coast	1-85937-259-7	£14.99
Luton (pb)	1-85937-235-x	£9.99	Surrey (pb)	1-85937-240-6	£9.99
Maidstone	1-85937-056-x	£14.99	Sussex (pb)	1-85937-184-1	£9.99
Manchester (pb)	1-85937-198-1	£9.99	Swansea (pb)	1-85937-167-1	£9.99
Middlesex	1-85937-158-2	£14.99	Tees Valley & Cleveland	1-85937-211-2	£14.99
New Forest	1-85937-128-0	£14.99	Thanet (pb)	1-85937-116-7	£9.99
Newark (pb)	1-85937-366-6	£9.99	Tiverton (pb)	1-85937-178-7	£9.99
Newport, Wales (pb)	1-85937-258-9	£9.99	Torbay	1-85937-063-2	£12.99
Newquay (pb)	1-85937-421-2	£9.99	Truro	1-85937-147-7	£12.99
Norfolk (pb)	1-85937-195-7	£9.99	Victorian and Edwardian Cornwall	1-85937-252-x	£14.99
Norfolk Living Memories	1-85937-217-1	£14.99	Victorian & Edwardian Devon	1-85937-253-8	£14.99
Northamptonshire	1-85937-150-7	£14.99	Victorian & Edwardian Kent	1-85937-149-3	£14.99
Northumberland Tyne & Wear (pb)	1-85937-281-3	£9.99	Vic & Ed Maritime Album	1-85937-144-2	£17.99
North Devon Coast	1-85937-146-9	£14.99	Victorian and Edwardian Sussex	1-85937-157-4	£14.99
North Devon Living Memories	1-85937-261-9	£14.99	Victorian & Edwardian Yorkshire	1-85937-154-x	£14.99
North London	1-85937-206-6	£14.99	Victorian Seaside	1-85937-159-0	£17.99
North Wales (pb)	1-85937-298-8	£9.99	Villages of Devon (pb)	1-85937-293-7	£9.99
North Yorkshire (pb)	1-85937-236-8	£9.99	Villages of Kent (pb)	1-85937-294-5	£9.99
Norwich (pb)	1-85937-194-9	£8.99	Villages of Sussex (pb)	1-85937-295-3	£9.99
Nottingham (pb)	1-85937-324-0	£9.99	Warwickshire (pb)	1-85937-203-1	£9.99
Nottinghamshire (pb)	1-85937-187-6	£9.99	Welsh Castles (pb)	1-85937-322-4	£9.99
Oxford (pb)	1-85937-411-5	£9.99	West Midlands (pb)	1-85937-289-9	£9.99
Oxfordshire (pb)	1-85937-430-1	£9.99	West Sussex	1-85937-148-5	£14.99
Peak District (pb)	1-85937-280-5	£9.99	West Yorkshire (pb)	1-85937-201-5	£9.99
Penzance	1-85937-069-1	£12.99	Weymouth (pb)	1-85937-209-0	£9.99
Peterborough (pb)	1-85937-219-8	£9.99	Wiltshire (pb)	1-85937-277-5	£9.99
Piers	1-85937-237-6	£17.99	Wiltshire Churches (pb)	1-85937-171-x	£9.99
Plymouth	1-85937-119-1	£12.99	Wiltshire Living Memories	1-85937-245-7	£14.99
Poole & Sandbanks (pb)	1-85937-251-1	£9.99	Winchester (pb)	1-85937-428-x	£9.99
Preston (pb)	1-85937-212-0	£9.99	Windmills & Watermills	1-85937-242-2	£17.99
Reading (pb)	1-85937-238-4	£9.99	Worcester (pb)	1-85937-165-5	£9.99
Romford (pb)	1-85937-319-4	£9.99	Worcestershire	1-85937-152-3	£14.99
Salisbury (pb)	1-85937-239-2	£9.99	York (pb)	1-85937-199-x	£9.99
Scarborough (pb)	1-85937-379-8	£9.99	Yorkshire (pb)	1-85937-186-8	£9.99
St Albans (pb)	1-85937-341-0	£9.99	Yorkshire Living Memories	1-85937-166-3	£14.99

See Frith books on the internet www.francisfrith.co.uk

FRITH PRODUCTS & SERVICES

Francis Frith would doubtless be pleased to know that the pioneering publishing venture he started in 1860 still continues today. A hundred and forty years later, The Francis Frith Collection continues in the same innovative tradition and is now one of the foremost publishers of vintage photographs in the world. Some of the current activities include:

Interior Decoration

Today Frith's photographs can be seen framed and as giant wall murals in thousands of pubs, restaurants, hotels, banks, retail stores and other public buildings throughout the country. In every case they enhance the unique local atmosphere of the places they depict and provide reminders of gentler days in an increasingly busy and frenetic world.

Product Promotions

Frith products are used by many major companies to promote the sales of their own products or to reinforce their own history and heritage. Frith promotions have been used by Hovis bread, Courage beers, Scots Porage Oats, Colman's mustard, Cadbury's foods, Mellow Birds coffee, Dunhill pipe tobacco, Guinness, and Bulmer's Cider.

Genealogy and Family History

As the interest in family history and roots grows world-wide, more and more people are turning to Frith's photographs of Great Britain for images of the towns, villages and streets where their ancestors lived; and, of course, photographs of the churches and chapels where their ancestors were christened, married and buried are an essential part of every genealogy tree and family album.

Frith Products

All Frith photographs are available Framed or just as Mounted Prints and Posters (size 23 x 16 inches). These may be ordered from the address below. From time to time other products - Address Books, Calendars, Table Mats, etc - are available.

The Internet

Already twenty thousand Frith photographs can be viewed and purchased on the internet through the Frith websites and a myriad of partner sites.

For more detailed information on Frith companies and products, look at these sites:

www.francisfrith.co.uk
www.francisfrith.com
(for North American visitors)

See the complete list of Frith Books at:

www.francisfrith.co.uk

This web site is regularly updated with the latest list of publications from the Frith Book Company. If you wish to buy books relating to another part of the country that your local bookshop does not stock, you may purchase on-line.

For further information, trade, or author enquiries please contact us at the address below:
The Francis Frith Collection, Frith's Barn, Teffont, Salisbury, Wiltshire, England SP3 5QP.
Tel: +44 (0)1722 716 376 Fax: +44 (0)1722 716 881 Email: sales@francisfrith.co.uk

See Frith books on the internet www.francisfrith.co.uk

TO RECEIVE YOUR FREE MOUNTED PRINT

Mounted Print
Overall size 14 x 11 inches

Cut out this Voucher and return it with your remittance for £1.95 to cover postage and handling, to UK addresses. For overseas addresses please include £4.00 post and handling. Choose any photograph included in this book. Your SEPIA print will be A4 in size, and mounted in a cream mount with burgundy rule line, overall size 14 x 11 inches.

Order additional Mounted Prints at HALF PRICE (only £7.49 each*)

If there are further pictures you would like to order, possibly as gifts for friends and family, purchase them at half price (no additional postage and handling required).

Have your Mounted Prints framed*

For an additional £14.95 per print you can have your chosen Mounted Print framed in an elegant polished wood and gilt moulding, overall size 16 x 13 inches (no additional postage and handling required).

> *** IMPORTANT!**
> These special prices are only available if ordered using the original voucher on this page (no copies permitted) and at the same time as your free Mounted Print, for delivery to the same address

Frith Collectors' Guild

From time to time we publish a magazine of news and stories about Frith photographs and further special offers of Frith products. If you would like 12 months FREE membership, please return this form.

Send completed forms to:
The Francis Frith Collection, Frith's Barn, Teffont, Salisbury, Wiltshire SP3 5QP

Voucher for FREE and Reduced Price Frith Prints

Picture no.	Page number	Qty	Mounted @ £7.49	Framed + £14.95	Total Cost
		1	**Free of charge***	£	£
			£7.49	£	£
			£7.49	£	£
			£7.49	£	£
			£7.49	£	£
			£7.49	£	£

Please allow 28 days for delivery   *** Post & handling**   £1.95

Book Title . . . .   **Total Order Cost**   £

Please do not photocopy this voucher. Only the original is valid, so please cut it out and return it to us.

I enclose a cheque / postal order for £ . . . .
made payable to 'The Francis Frith Collection'
OR please debit my Mastercard / Visa / Switch / Amex card
(credit cards please on all overseas orders)

Number . . . .

Issue No(Switch only) . . . . .Valid from (Amex/Switch) . . . .

Expires . . . .   Signature . . . .

Name Mr/Mrs/Ms . . . .

Address . . . .

. . . .

. . . . Postcode . . . .

Daytime Tel No . . . .   Valid to 31/12/02

The Francis Frith Collectors' Guild

Please enrol me as a member for 12 months free of charge.

Name Mr/Mrs/Ms . . . .

Address . . . .

. . . .

. . . . Postcode . . . .

Would you like to find out more about Francis Frith?

We have recently recruited some entertaining speakers who are happy to visit local groups, clubs and societies to give an illustrated talk documenting Frith's travels and photographs. If you are a member of such a group and are interested in hosting a presentation, we would love to hear from you.

Our speakers bring with them a small selection of our local town and county books, together with sample prints. They are happy to take orders. A small proportion of the order value is donated to the group who have hosted the presentation. The talks are therefore an excellent way of fundraising for small groups and societies.

Can you help us with information about any of the Frith photographs in this book?

We are gradually compiling an historical record for each of the photographs in the Frith archive. It is always fascinating to find out the names of the people shown in the pictures, as well as insights into the shops, buildings and other features depicted.

If you recognize anyone in the photographs in this book, or if you have information not already included in the author's caption, do let us know. We would love to hear from you, and will try to publish it in future books or articles.

Our production team

Frith books are produced by a small dedicated team at offices in the converted Grade II listed 18th-century barn at Teffont near Salisbury, illustrated above. Most have worked with the Frith Collection for many years. All have in common one quality: they have a passion for the Frith Collection. The team is constantly expanding, but currently includes:

Jason Buck, John Buck, Douglas Burns, Heather Crisp, Isobel Hall, Rob Hames, Hazel Heaton, Peter Horne, James Kinnear, Tina Leary, Hannah Marsh, Eliza Sackett, Terence Sackett, Sandra Sanger, Shelley Tolcher, Susanna Walker, Clive Wathen and Jenny Wathen.

3. 00

URBAN ARBOREAL

A MODERN GLOSSARY OF CITY TREES

Michael Jordan and
Kelly Louise Judd

WHITE
LION
PUBLISHING

CONTENTS

INTRODUCTION

'Trees are the lungs of the earth'. It's a sentiment that is more romantic than scientifically accurate, but it contains an important grain of truth in that trees and other green plants generate the vital oxygen without which we would not survive. They do so by a far-from-simple natural process known as photosynthesis, during which carbon dioxide and water, drawn from the air and soil, are merged chemically using the energy of sunlight, to produce the sugars on which green plants live and grow. There is, however, a further essential ingredient in this process, oxygen, which the plants discharge as a superfluous by-product. Therein lies one of the indispensible miracles of nature that determines our future survival on this planet. All living things give off harmful carbon dioxide through their respiration, which would otherwise build up to lethal levels. But green plants not only absorb this gas during photosynthesis, removing it from the atmosphere, they also release oxygen in the process.

Pollution from motor vehicles and other industrial sources that burn fossil fuels like coal, oil and natural gas, constantly discharges carbon dioxide into the atmosphere. It has now become a serious problem in most of the world's towns and cities, and one vital way in which urban pollution is being tackled is through the planting of trees. In an average year of growth a mature oak or lime tree, planted on a roadside verge, will not only absorb large amounts of carbon dioxide but it will also produce more than 100kg/220lbs of oxygen.

Yet urban tree planting is not without its problems and drawbacks. Many tree species are simply unable to tolerate the high levels of pollution that have now been reached in most of the world's conurbations. One of the more notable exceptions is the so-called London plane tree, which of any tree species has just about the strongest resistance to pollution. For this reason it tends to be a popular urban selection in the temperate regions of both hemispheres.

The variety of trees that can be planted in urban areas can be further restricted by issues such as shallow spreading root systems, strong enough that they will readily undermine and lift tarmac, and even solid concrete. The same roots may also disrupt and fracture water supplies and drainage systems. Then there is the not-insignificant matter of wind-resistance and vulnerability to storm damage. Beech trees, which in many respects might seem ideal for urban planting, tend not to be a popular choice because not only are their boughs brittle and prone to shedding without notice, but their root systems are sufficiently shallow to make them potentially unstable in any kind of excessive wind speed.

Trees also behave differently in contrasting habitats. When packed tightly together in a modern forestry plantation they will tend to grow tall, straight and narrow, quite unlike their more broadly arranged counterparts growing in an open, natural woodland setting. The same will often be true of sidewalk trees planted in the deep, shadowy canyons between modern high-rise buildings. They will grow thin and spindly, searching upwards for light, but when planted on an open airy roadside verge, the same species is likely to behave more as nature intended, growing broadly and densely enough to obscure visibility for passing traffic, and creating a potentially dangerous obstacle to high-sided vehicles. Larger tree species may also impact on nearby power lines. These are all considerations that must be taken into account when deciding which species to plant in towns and cities, and where to plant them. The tree that may be ideal for the urban park may not present quite such a good choice for lining the adjacent high street.

Urban tree-planting now earns its own buzz-phrase: the 'greening' of cities, and major programmes of planting are currently gaining pace around the planet. The policy has benefits that extend far beyond the curbing of urban pollution. Trees make urban areas more scenically attractive places in which to live and work, they provide shade from the sun's heat, often at its most oppressive in the 'concrete jungle'. They also provide essential food and refuge for wildlife. Without trees the number of species of birds frequenting our urban and industrial areas would rapidly be reduced to scarcely more than those ubiquitous pigeons and sparrows.

Trees are one of the most precious assets that we have on our fragile planet Earth. Without them, whether they reach upwards towards the sky in a distant forest, or in the centre of the metropolis, we too cease to exist.

Acer rubrum
Red maple
New York

The vibrant autumn colours of the red maple are irresistible. The species is indigenous to large parts of eastern and central North America, and it is actually named by the US Forest Service as the most abundant native tree in the United States. It is possible to find red maple gracing streets and parks more or less anywhere in New York, and in autumn, it is clearly the chief attention-grabber. Perhaps less well known, in springtime it provides a dazzling though very transient delicate red blossom. The spectacle lasts barely more than a few days, but its short period of finery is definitely worth catching. One of the first trees to bloom in early spring, red maple is easy to spot along the streets of Brooklyn, the Bronx and Queens, though it is less plentiful in Manhattan. Seeking them out in some of the city's parks, especially Mosholu Parkway, Pelham Parkway and Van Cortlandt Park, is also rewarding.

Acer rubrum is variable in appearance and size. The largest known living red maple (located in New Jersey) has reached a height of 38m/125ft, but generally the tree will grow to between 18–27m/59–89ft, extending at less than 1m/3ft a year. The canopy achieves a spread of about 12m/39ft, displaying characteristic whip-like upturned reddish twigs. The trunk is clothed with smooth, pale grey bark when young, becoming darker and fissured with age. The deciduous leaves are palmate, widely lobed and with toothed margins, turning a brilliant red in autumn. Male and female flowers emerge before the leaves, in separate clusters (and usually on different trees), at any time from late January to May. They are unusual in that they can sometimes switch from male to female to being hermaphrodite. The winged fruits are red and borne in pairs on a long slender stalk.

Acer rubrum should not, however, be confused with *Acer saccharum* (sugar maple), from which maple syrup is made, and which in 1956 was adopted as an emblem of New York State. The latter species is no less beautiful but has not been found to be as well suited to urban planting.

ACER RUBRUM

Acer saccharinum
Silver maple
Warsaw

The city of Warsaw is not celebrated chiefly for its urban trees. One of the prettiest and most frequently planted, however, has been *Acer saccharinum*, which is, incidentally, a species distinct from *Acer saccharum* (sugar maple). A monumental silver maple of uncertain age stands in Kisielewski Square, near the botanic garden, and is not to be missed. At a height of about 25m/82ft, it has achieved a girth of more than 4.5m/15ft, and its spread at the crown is a remarkable 28m/92ft. Leaning at what appears to be a slightly precarious angle, it carries a number of bracket fungi on its main trunk but seems to remain healthy. Alas, many of the silver maples that once graced the streets of Warsaw have been lost or are in poor condition. This is mainly because the species is intolerant of the high salinity levels that result from frequent de-icing of roads, but also due to air pollution caused by the traffic fumes in busy thoroughfares. Happily, they are still well represented in the city's parks. In Lazienki Park, which covers 76 hectares/188 acres in the heart of Warsaw, they provide an attractive autumnal backdrop to the famous Chopin statue. There are also some fine specimen trees to be discovered in Skaryszewski Park, a short walk across the Vistula.

Silver maple is indigenous to eastern and central North America, but it has long been popular as an ornamental and can be found in many temperate parts of the world. It is a fairly fast-growing deciduous tree that can reach a height of 25m/82ft, occasionally more, attaining a spread of 11–15m/36–49ft. The bark is smooth and grey in young trees, but becomes increasingly roughened with age. It bears palmate leaves with five lobes separated by deep, jagged notches. The tree earns the popular name 'silver maple' because the undersides of the leaves are clothed with silvery down, and even in a light breeze the effect can be magical. In autumn, the leaves generally display soft yellow and gold tints. The flowers appear in small inconspicuous clusters in early spring, and the fruits are winged samaras. Silver and red maple, incidentally, are the only *Acer* species that fruit in springtime, before the leaves have fully developed.

The silver maple owes much of its popularity to its adaptability, although it does require more sunlight than some other species of maple trees.

ACER SACCHARINUM

Aesculus hippocastanum
Horse chestnut
Paris

You need to be in Paris in April or May if you want to see the horse chestnuts flowering at their showy best along the city's grand boulevards. They look magnificent, as if studded with great white candles. One of the largest trees in the capital is an impressive 200-year-old horse chestnut standing beside a lake in the Avenue Gustave Eiffel, close to the base of the Eiffel Tower itself. Planted sometime between 1814 and 1820, it is about 22m/72ft tall and boasts a girth of nearly 6m/20ft. Another veteran, rather smaller and a mere 3m/10ft in girth, dwells in the grounds of the Rodin Museum, near the Hôtel des Invalides. Out in the Buttes-Chaumont Park, you will find an extraordinary specimen angled over a pathway at about 45 degrees from the vertical. How it survives is something of a mystery. There is an abundance of horse chestnuts in the Tuileries Gardens, and in the Père Lachaise Cemetery they cast their shade over the graves of the famous.

This impressive, broadly spreading deciduous tree is native to mountains in the Balkan Peninsula. It can reach 30m/100ft or more in height. In springtime it develops large upright clusters of bee-pollinated flowers at the tips of the branches; and in the heat of summer, the massive rounded canopy, clothed with broad, palmate leaves, provides welcome shade. At the onset of autumn, the glossy reddish-brown nuts begin to mature, preparing to fall from their spiky green shells. As a fast-growing tree, tolerant of a range of climatic conditions and a degree of traffic pollution, it has been popular for planting along urban avenues and in parks and ornamental gardens. Sadly, not only in Paris but also across Europe, these lovely trees are under threat from a variety of modern diseases, due both to leaf-mining moths and bacterial pests, for which there are no effective controls other than felling.

The tree gains its common name because of a bygone fallacy that horses ate the nuts, which allegedly cured them of respiratory complaints. The notion was strengthened by the fact that when the leaves fall, they leave a scar on the twig resembling a horseshoe. The nuts are, in reality, poisonous.

AESCULUS HIPPOCASTANUM

Ailanthus altissima
Tree of heaven
Wiesbaden

The Spa Park in Wiesbaden was created in 1852, and a number of species planted at that time have now become magnificent veterans. The park's impressive tree of heaven was actually introduced a little later, probably in the 1930s. Nonetheless it has almost reached the considerable height of 26m/85ft, with a girth of nearly 3m/10ft. It appears to be one of the biggest living examples worldwide, although there are others that have achieved even greater proportions, including one in Vienna that is about 31m/102ft tall. The species enjoys a moderate longevity; the oldest known *Ailanthus altissima* alive today is reckoned to be aged more than 150 years.

Why 'tree of heaven'? The origin seems to rest in the corruption of an Indonesian word 'ailanto', which means 'tree reaching for the sky' and is attributable to its very rapid growth. Also known as the Chinese sumac, and the copal tree, it is native to a region of northern and central China, but has proved to be a fairly invasive species. The first specimens found their way into Europe via England where they were introduced in 1751. It was taken across the Atlantic to North America by a gardener named William Hamilton in 1784, and has since then spread extensively as far as Canada.

This deciduous tree has a very rapid rate of growth and a typical height of 15–20m/49–66ft. It bears large pinnate leaves, each carrying up to twenty-five broadly ovate, pointed leaflets, which have a reddish tinge when young. Distinctive dot-like glands can be seen at the lower edge of the leaflets. The pale grey bark is smooth to the touch, but when the timber is cut it gives off a foetid odour. Female trees produce long, pyramidal clusters of tiny greenish-yellow flowers in late spring. Male flowers, also greenish, are borne on separate trees and emanate an unpleasant smell. The winged, propeller-like fruits mature in autumn in prolific numbers: a tree can discharge more than 300,000 seeds in a single season. These are dispersed by wind, but are also buoyant enough to float on water.

The tree produces toxins which can get into the soil and prevent the establishment of other plant species, leading a number of concerned botanists worldwide to suggest that a more appropriate name might be 'tree of hell'.

AILANTHUS ALTISSIMA

Albizia julibrissin
Persian silk tree
Barcelona

It is to the credit of a Florentine nobleman, Filippo degli Albizzi, that this delightful tree was first introduced to Europe in the mid-18th century. Its native range lies in southwestern and eastern Asia, extending from Iran to China and Japan. Today more than 1,100 Persian silk trees grace the city of Barcelona, where it is also known by the curious title 'acacia of Constantinople'. One of the finest veteran specimens is to be discovered in the Ciutadella Park located in the Ciutat Vella or old city. Planted in 1896, the tree has reached a height of nearly 12m/39ft, although during its long life it has suffered from a series of infections that have hollowed out part of its trunk. Les Corts Park, on the Carrer de Numància, is also worth exploring as it contains a considerable variety of trees for its size, including *Albizia julibrissin*. The Cervantes Park, to be found between Avinguda Diagonal and Ronda de Dalt, has other fine specimens.

Albizia julibrissin is a medium-sized deciduous tree with a comparatively short lifespan, largely because it is prone to fungal disease. It rarely grows to more than 10m/33ft in the wild, but displays a broad profile up to 8m/26ft across. The trunk is often sloping or distorted, and the smooth bark is grey or light brown. The compound leaves are 20–45cm/8–18in long and finely divided into deep-green leaflets, not dissimilar to those of an acacia, with paler undersides. The leaves possess a curious property that allows them to close up not only at dusk, but also when it rains, looking as if they have fallen asleep, and this lends it another common name, the 'sleeping tree'. But the flowers are the real glory of the Persian silk tree, emerging between June and September. Their most striking feature, coupled with the virtual lack of visible petals, lies in the tubular clusters of intensely pink and white stamens, up to 15cm/6in long. The fruit is a flattened brown pod of 7–20cm/2¾–8in that hangs down from the branch.

ALBIZIA JULIBRISSIN

Aleurites moluccanus
Candlenut
Honolulu

It may not be common knowledge, but this is one of several trees from which blossom and leaves are gathered in order to make the famous *lei* of Hawaii. Also known as *kukui*, it has long been revered as a symbol of peace and enlightenment, and in 1959 it became the state tree of Hawaii. The species is not a native of Hawaii, but was introduced at some time in the distant past from Polynesia, and is now a common sight across the tropical Pacific region and in parts of Africa. Aside from its ceremonial significance, it has considerable economic value and is a popular ornamental. The trees can be found growing more or less anywhere in Honolulu and the surrounding Hawaiian Islands. There are some pretty examples in the grounds of the Foster Botanical Garden, and if you don't mind a gentle hike, there is also a candlenut grove in the Diamond Head Crater, just off Diamond Head Road.

Aleurites moluccanus is an evergreen tree that can achieve a height of 20m/66ft, borne up on a slim trunk with a diameter of slightly less than 1m/3ft. It has fairly irregular branches that tend to droop close to the ground and form a widely spreading canopy. The leaves are a distinctive silvery green (due to a dense covering of hairs) and range in length from 10–20cm/4–8in. They are either lobed or a more regular oval to triangular shape. The creamy-white flowers are held in showy clusters that reveal an unusual structure: each female flower is surrounded by a number of small male flowers. The fruit that results from fertilisation is a drupe containing a seed that appears not unlike that of a walnut.

The tree is known as the candlenut because a type of candlestick has traditionally been created from the nuts, which can be strung on the stiff midrib of a palm leaf and burnt from one end. Oil extracted from the nuts is also used in stone lamps, and the nuts were also burnt and powdered to make the ink employed in traditional tattooing.

ALEURITES MOLUCCANUS

Aquilaria sinensis
Incense tree
Hong Kong

Once widely planted in the city as a source of raw material for incense production, to the extent that the Chinese name *Hong Kong* means fragrant harbour or incense harbour, sadly this tree is now facing severe threat from illegal exploitation, and steps are being taken by the Hong Kong authorities to protect it. Illegal harvesting of the timber has resulted in the loss of many of Hong Kong's oldest and biggest incense trees. As a countermeasure, the species is now listed as being vulnerable under the CITES convention and police patrols are on the lookout specifically for incense tree loggers. New trees are being planted in inner city areas such as West Kowloon's central park, while there is a policy in the surrounding countryside to plant in the order of 10,000 seedlings annually. In the northern suburbs, near the Chinese border, the last of Hong Kong's commercial plantations is zealously guarded. Mature trees, also under close protection, can be found in small woodlands associated with many of the older villages and temples. There are thought be about 100 mature incense trees left in Hong Kong. Needless to say, the locations are not advertised.

Aquilaria sinensis is an evergreen tree indigenous to China, found mainly in monsoon forests at altitudes of up to 400m/1,312ft. It grows to a height of about 20m/66ft, narrowly triangular in profile and sparsely branched when young, clothed with smooth and greyish bark. The leathery, ovate leaves are 5–11cm/2¼–4¼in long, with entire margins. The pretty flowers are gathered into little clusters or umbels. Small, yellowish-green and fragrant, they open at night from April to May and are pollinated by moths. The fruit is an elongated green capsule that becomes woody at maturity and splits open to release the seeds.

The timber, the popularity of which has been the cause of so much damage to the stocks of trees in China and Hong Kong, is fragrant, sought-after for making ornaments, and, going under its local Chinese name *Chen Xiang*, it is also highly prized in herbal medicine. A policy of regeneration in mainland China has now resulted in the planting of over one million five-year-old trees.

AQUILARIA SINENSIS

Araucaria araucana
Monkey puzzle
Santiago

This extraordinary-looking conifer, Chile's national tree, is now a rare sight outside the country's forest reserves. Otherwise known as the Chilean pine, it is indigenous to central and southern Chile and the western parts of Argentina. However, it is under threat of extinction and its population in the wild is dwindling, to the extent that in 1971 it became protected by law. Perhaps not surprisingly, very few are to be found in the capital city. However, some striking specimens do exist within the urban confines, if you know where to look! A pair of fine, comparatively youthful specimens stand together in a small green oasis named Augusto Errázuriz Park, in the Providencia district. The recently renovated park can be discovered at the intersection of Avenida Pocuro and Avenida Tobalaba, and is well worth a visit if only to admire these fabulous forms, still displaying a beautiful, bullet-shaped profile that dominates the skyline.

Chilean pine is an evergreen tree, the native range of which is restricted to the Andean mountain slopes, typically above 1,000m/3,280ft. It grows to a height of 30–40m/100–130ft on a slender trunk about 1.5m/5ft in diameter. The trunk eventually becomes devoid of branches apart from a spreading, dome-shaped crown. The distinctively stalkless, triangular leaves are thick and tough, with a scaly appearance. Each leaf is thought to have a lifespan of around twenty years. The tree itself is capable of great longevity, bearing seeds only after thirty to forty years, and potentially surviving for more than a 1,000 years. Pollination is by wind. Male cones are oblong, shaped rather like cucumbers. Female cones, borne on separate trees, are more rounded, each containing about 200 seeds. These ripen after eighteen months or so, are released when the cones disintegrate while still on the bough, and are then mainly dispersed by rodents.

Logging of the trees is now banned, but in 2002 fires destroyed large sections of native araucaria forest, including specimens known to be more than 1,300 years old. 'Monkey puzzle' is an English name coined in about 1850 when the species was still rare in European gardens. On seeing a young tree in Cornwall, a noted barrister of the day remarked, 'It would puzzle a monkey to climb that!'

ARAUCARIA ARAUCANA

Arbutus unedo
Strawberry tree
Madrid

Known in Spain as *el madroño*, this is the European counterpart of the Pacific madrone, native to the west coast of America. *El madroño* is such a quintessential feature of the Spanish capital that since the 13th century the city's coat of arms has featured a bear standing on its hind legs, eating fruit from the tree. Tree and bear are everywhere! There is a charming bronze and stone sculpture on the east side of Puerta del Sol Square in the city centre, depicting the bear munching away. The same imagery, in low relief, is carved on the Alcachofa Fountain in Retiro Park. You can even find it on manhole covers, corporation dustbins and the shirt of Atlético Madrid. Though it is suggested that some Madrileños have never actually seen either in the flesh, a sad consequence perhaps of too many Spanish bears being shot and too many strawberry trees being chopped up for firewood. The species tends to be found in parts of the city where there is scrubby wasteland, and it grows extensively throughout Madrid province, at altitudes of up to 750m/2,460ft. Unusually, it flowers just as the previous year's fruits reach full ripeness; to coincide with this moment, you need to visit Madrid in November.

Arbutus unedo is evergreen, and is as much a large shrub as a tree, bearing broad, glossy leaves on red stems. It is a member of the heather family, which may seem surprising until you see the clusters of familiar bell-shaped greenish-white or pinkish flowers. The ripe fruits resemble strawberries in colour and shape (hence the tree's common name). The fruit has a scent reminiscent of aniseed but, sadly, tastes bland and uninteresting – although it has a tendency to ferment on the branch, and if eaten can cause mild intoxication! The rough bark produces tannins that were once used in the leather industry.

For reasons that are unclear, but which must be accountable to some botanical migration now lost to distant history, *Arbutus unedo* is also to be found growing wild in woodlands near Killarney, in southwest Ireland, from where it was introduced to England. For the Romans, the tree was thought to possess magical powers – because of fruit and flowers appearing together – and this may explain the custom of laying sprigs of *Arbutus* on graves.

ARBUTUS UNEDO

Artocarpus altilis
Breadfruit tree
Honolulu

Breadfruit has been cultivated in and around Honolulu, the city on the southern coast of Oahu, for about a thousand years, and prior to the coming of modern influences and eating habits, the breadfruit was a significant part of a Hawaiian's diet. The trees do not commonly grace roadsides in the city, but they are a fairly common site in private gardens, and across the Hawaiian Islands there are specimen trees to be discovered in several ornamental gardens open to the public. One of the more pleasant spots in which to find mature breadfruit is in Honolulu's Foster Botanical Garden. This covers 5.7 hectares/14 acres in the centre of Honolulu and is home to over 4,000 tropical species. In Bernice Street, in the city's Kalihi district, another well-preserved breadfruit tree can be discovered at the Bishop Museum. There are also fine specimens located in the National Tropical Botanic Garden on the east coast of Maui, and in the Hawaii Tropical Botanical Garden on the east coast of Hawaii Island.

Artocarpus altilis is a fast-growing evergreen or semi-deciduous tree that can reach a height of 26m/85ft. It has a straight trunk with low, spreading branches that give it value as a shade tree. It bears thick, often deeply dissected leaves. Male and female flowers are carried on the same tree in the axils of the leaves. The male flowers are very small with a single stamen and droop on long stalks. The females are more obvious, and are upright and cylindrical, or somewhat rounded. The fruit, which results from the fertilisation of multiple flowers in a single inflorescence, is greenish-yellow and up to 30cm/12in in diameter, with a fleshy, juicy pulp and a surface resembling that of a knobbly lemon. The varieties in cultivation are generally seedless; others produce seeds in vast numbers that largely replace the flesh. An individual tree can yield more than 200 breadfruits in a season.

The species has now been naturalised and cultivated with innumerable cultivars throughout the tropics, and is a staple crop on many of the islands of Polynesia and Micronesia.

ARTOCARPUS ALTILIS

Betula pendula
Silver birch
Helsinki

Along with conifers, the silver birch conjures up vivid images of chilly northern landscapes. It has been Finland's national emblem since 1988, when it won a popular vote. Yet, for a country of birch forests, Finland can claim very few monumental examples. The main reason for this paucity stems back to pagan times. Finland was among the last countries of Europe to adopt Christianity, and pagan Finns worshipped trees, often the bigger ones. To combat this practice, the emergent Christian establishment ordered many iconic trees to be cut down. Fortunately, in spite of the former purges, today Helsinki is not short of its birch trees. Numerous roads and walkways are today lined with silver birch, and young trees grace many of the urban parks. One truly splendid mature specimen can be discovered in the Kaisaniemi Botanic Garden, though its age and dimensions are not recorded. Around the city you will also encounter birches with special plaques. These are part of a Sibelius tree walk, created in 2015 for the 150th anniversary of the composer's birth: by scanning the tree's QR code you can listen to the music it inspired.

The most distinctive feature of the silver birch, clothing all but the young twigs, is the flaking silvery bark, punctuated by dark horseshoe-shaped scars. The branches of this deciduous tree, which can reach a height of about 25m/82ft, extend characteristically in a graceful, drooping fashion. The leaves are small, notched and triangular in outline. In springtime, the boughs become decorated with dangly male catkins popularly called lamb's tails, and more upright, wind-pollinated females. The cone-like fruit disintegrates to release small winged seeds. This species is closely related to downy birch (*Betula pubescens*), also a common sight in Helsinki, and whose bark does not flake. In both, the young leaves are very soft but in downy birch they are also rather furry, for which reason they have attracted the local Finnish name of 'mouse ears'.

Birch timber constitutes a major industrial resource in Finland, providing raw material for paper-making, furniture and construction. Many of the country's older houses are built from birch wood. Birch bark was also once used in roofing or woven to create shoes, and the sap was extracted as a tonic. On Midsummer's Day Finns still stand two silver birch saplings outside their doorways for good luck.

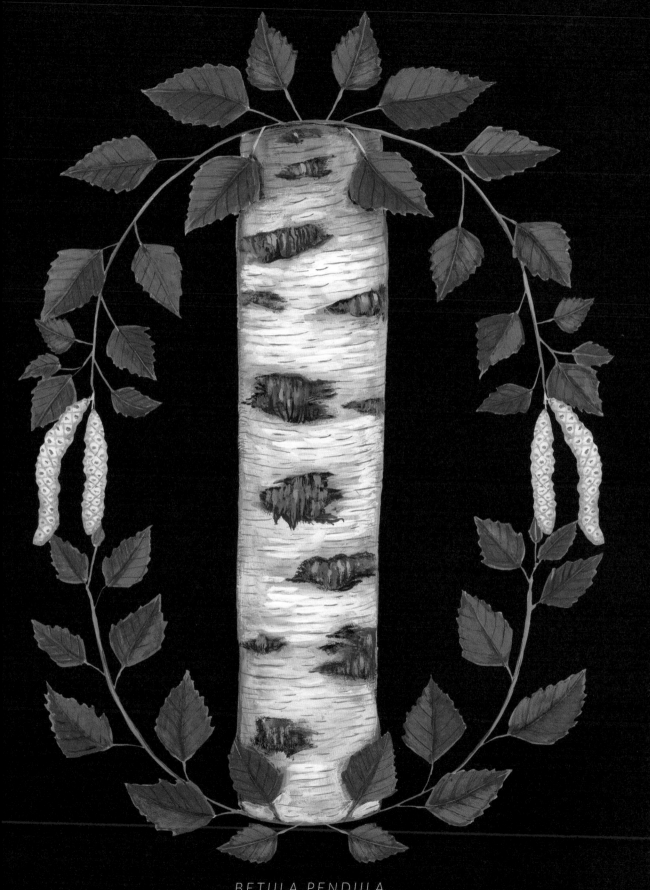

BETULA PENDULA

Cassia fistula
Amaltas
New Delhi

This glorious flowering tree, also known as Indian laburnum, is a vision to delight the eye when in full bloom, and is well worth seeking out around the streets of Delhi. Ideal starting places include the urban avenues of Panchsheel Marg and Amrita Shergil Marg, where the trees have been planted along the length of the streets. They also grow extensively along both sides of Hailey Road in central Delhi. Away from the bustle of traffic, at Shakti Sthal, they provide a backdrop to the memorial of Indira Gandhi – who was assassinated in 1984 while serving as prime minister – reached by the Kashmiri Gate metro station.

Native to the Indian subcontinent and parts of southeast Asia, this species from the bean family is a moderately sized, fairly drought-tolerant tree, preferring life in full sun and well-drained soil. It is fast-growing to a maximum height of 20m/66ft, with a broadly spreading deciduous canopy of large pinnate leaves, each with three to eight pairs of leaflets. The fruit is a large pod up to 60cm/24in long. There are several cultivars predominantly bearing yellow flowers, although some varieties display purple flowers. The blooms erupt in March and April, have a mild scent and reach into the topmost branches of the tree, almost wholly obscuring the leaves. Each flower consists of five yellow petals of equal size revealing long curving stamens, with pollination by bees and butterflies. The flowers are comparatively short-lived, however, and within a few days are falling more or less continuously onto the pavements below, forming a thick golden carpet, a reason that the tree has gained the popular name 'golden shower'. It was the annual mess caused by leaf and flower fall that made it a less than firm favourite street tree with the British raj. Nonetheless it managed to earn and maintain its place in Delhi.

The tree has a long history of use in herbal medicine to alleviate a variety of ailments. One of its many names is the purging cassia, and it is often cultivated in India purely for medicinal use.

CASSIA FISTULA

Cassia surattensis
Golden senna
Cairo

Date palms are not the only species to grace the streets of Cairo. Smaller, but decidedly prettier, is the golden senna. It is also known more prosaically as the scrambled egg tree, because when in bloom it is covered all over with brilliant yellow flowers. The effect is extraordinarily beautiful. It is also one of those intriguing plants in which the leaves are light-sensitive. At sunset they relax and fold downward, reopening again in the morning. *Senna surattensis* copes well with Egypt's semi-tropical climate, where it has become increasingly popular as a roadside tree, to the extent that in some places it risks being seen as an invasive weed. During the flowering season it is not hard to find throughout the urban areas of Cairo, and is equally common in Giza and Luxor.

The tree grows rapidly to a maximum height of 4–7m/13–23ft, with a lifespan of twenty-five to fifty years. It can form a multi-stemmed shrub, branching from ground level; but when grown on a single trunk it develops a fine, airy canopy that is often fairly irregular in profile. The greyish bark soon becomes finely cracked. Partly evergreen, it develops pinnate leaves consisting of four to nine pairs of dark green oval leaflets. Flowers appear in springtime, clustered in rounded panicles in the leaf axils, and can persist over quite a long period. Each bloom bears five showy petals surrounding both male and female parts. Although insect-pollinated, the flowers are devoid of scent. The fruits are flattened, elongated pods typical of the bean family. They hang straight down from the branches; at first green, they become brown when ripe.

This species is native to southeast Asia but its precise range is uncertain as it has been cultivated in tropical regions for so long. In traditional medicine, an extract of the flowers is commonly relied on as a herbal treatment for various ailments, including the fungal disease aspergillosis. An infusion of senna leaves (distinct from the pods) is also employed therapeutically, and has sometimes been described as a miracle herb.

CASSIA SURATTENSIS

Castanea sativa
Sweet chestnut
Piancastagnaio

Italy is famous for many things, but one of the country's assets that may sometimes go unnoticed is its chestnut trees. They can be found in and around towns and cities from Sicily northwards to Turin, and one of the most picturesque is the Tuscan hilltop town of Piancastagnaio. It lies south of Siena on the slopes of Mount Amiata, where sweet chestnuts have been cultivated since the 14th century as one of the few sources of sustenance that can be grown successfully in this mountainous area. The town's name means 'place of chestnuts' and, not surprisingly, its emblem is a chestnut tree, so you get the impression that *Castanea sativa* is fairly important there! A magnificent grove stands in the town centre, in a little park beside the Aldobrandesca Fortress. There is also a centuries-old veteran by the church of San Bartolomeo, on the road in from Abbadia San Salvatore. So revered are the trees that in the last week of October Piancastagnaio holds *Il Crastatone*, an autumn festival in honour of the sweet chestnut.

Indigenous to southern Europe, western Asia and north Africa, *Castanea sativa* is a deciduous tree that can present an awesome spectacle when it attains full size. Reaching 35m/115ft at maturity, its vast, gnarled trunk becomes deeply carved with a network of fissures that sometimes forms a spiral pattern. The jaggedly distorted branches create an equally massive, broad canopy with limbs that sweep close to the ground. The ovate leaves, up to 28cm/11in long, have pointed tips and toothed edges. Long yellow catkins appear in midsummer; each consists predominantly of male flowers, with the females located at the base. Trees do not bear fruit until they are about twenty-five years old. The fruit takes the form of a spiny green husk enclosing the familiar, shiny reddish-brown chestnuts.

Renowned for their longevity, sweet chestnut trees can live for 700 years or more. The Romans relied on chestnuts as a source of coarse flour when cereal grain was in short supply, and were largely responsible for the introduction of the tree into other parts of the Roman Empire.

CASTANEA SATIVA

Casuarina cunninghamiana
River oak
Canberra

Indigenous throughout much of eastern Australia, from northern Queensland to southern New South Wales, this species is found across a wide strip that extends inland from the coast for about 400km/250mi. While river oak favours the margins of freshwater rivers and streams in its native habitat, it is now fairly commonly planted in the Canberra area. Take a stroll down City Walk to see some fine specimens. These have grown taller and thinner than usual due to the shade of nearby buildings, but trees with a more familiar silhouette can be found in Solander Place, located off Banks Street, and in the Yarralumla district. River oaks feature in the Commonwealth Park and neighbouring Kings Park, between Parkes Way and the Molonglo River. Northwest from the city centre, there are good examples in the Gossan Hill Nature Reserve, adjacent to the University of Canberra's main campus. A little further out, on the city's southern outskirts, lies Point Hut Pond with an attractive surrounding of mature river oaks.

In the wild, the mature trees can grow up to 35m/115ft in height, though in cultivation they generally achieve 18–20m/59–66ft. Also known as Australian beefwood (and no relation of true oaks), the species develops a rounded to elliptical profile, up to 15m/49ft in width, borne on a sturdy trunk clothed in finely fissured grey bark. It is evergreen but the leaves are virtually non-existent, replaced by slender, slightly pendulous dark green branchlets. The male and female flowers, held on separate trees, are insignificant. The females form a small, woody, cone-like structure and produce winged seeds that are readily dispersed by both wind and water.

As an urban planting, the river oak can cope with amounts of air and salt pollution and with compacted soils. It is less tolerant, however, of drought conditions. The trees provide a valuable source of food for a range of wildlife, and are listed as being ecologically beneficial under the Australian Tree Protection Act of 2005. Having a smooth bark and a high water content, river oak is also considered to be fire retardant in a region where summer bush fires are common.

CASUARINA
CUNNINGHAMIANA

Cedrus atlantica
Atlas cedar
Turin

Some fine Atlas cedars can be discovered close to the centre of Turin, where the vast and beautiful Valentino Park hugs the west bank of the River Po. These, however, have not achieved the awesome dimensions of specimen trees, the sight of which can reward those prepared to travel a short distance out of the city. One of the most glorious veterans of any in cultivation is to be discovered at Villa Michelini, in Turin's Perosa Canavese northern municipality. It is thought to have been planted in about 1830, and at about 30m/100ft in height the tree is colossal by any standards. Having developed multiple trunks, it has achieved a girth of more than 12m/39ft, dwarfing anyone standing at its base. An equally breathtaking cedar can be spied in the grounds of a private villa in the nearby village of Montalenghe.

The home of *Cedrus atlantica*, as one of its common names suggests, lies in the Atlas Mountains of Algeria and Morocco. In its native surroundings the tree can reach a height of 40m/130ft, although those reared in cultivation rarely exceed 30m/100ft. Evergreen, it bears distinctively short needles that spread rosette-wise in little whorls. These vary naturally in colour from dark green to a glaucous blue. In cultivation, the blue-leaved variants are known collectively as the Glauca Group. The branches tilt slightly upwards and thin out towards the crown. The female cones, which appear in the upper branches, are cylindrical, pointing upwards, and they do not mature until their second year. *Cedrus atlantica* can be confused with *Cedrus libani*, the Cedar of Lebanon, but the branches of that tree do not angle upwards.

The magnificent blue Atlas cedar has become a much-loved ornamental tree. There is one celebrated example on the South Lawn of the White House, planted by America's seventh president, Andrew Jackson. But it was probably from around 1945 that this colour variant really began to gain popularity and its commercial cultivation took off.

CEDRUS ATLANTICA

Ceiba pentandra
Cotton tree
Freetown

On a roundabout near the Supreme Court building in Freetown's busy city centre, known locally as the *kapok*, this tree has become a national symbol for Sierra Leone. At a height of 30m/100ft, the tree dominates the urban skyline and is reputed to be 500 years old, though is probably somewhat younger. In 2017 Freetown suffered a devastating mudslide from adjacent Sugar Loaf mountain, resulting in major loss of life and property, but the specimen tree remained unscathed and has now become famous. Perhaps predictably, romantic stories – including tales of magical properties – about its history abound. It is said that the city's founders, freed slaves who journeyed from Nova Scotia, held a thanksgiving service under the tree after disembarking from their ship, and later settled on the site of the modern city; whether true or false, Sierra Leoneans still pray and leave offerings to ancestors beneath the tree.

Ceiba pentandra is indigenous both to west Africa and to parts of tropical America (but is not to be confused with *Bombax ceiba*, the red cotton tree of tropical Asia). A giant by any standards, it is reputedly the tallest deciduous species on either continent. In tropical rainforests it can reach a height of over 60m/200ft, with a buttressed trunk that can spread out massively in girth. The branches extend horizontally in tiered whorls and are armed, as is the trunk, with sharp thorns. The long-stalked palmate leaves, each with five to eight leaflets, fall in the dry season, and flowers emerge while the tree is bare. The showy, five-petalled whitish-pink flowers each have five slender stamens that fan out from the centre. The tree blooms at night: pollination is by insects and bats. The resultant fruit is an elongated capsule with a coarse grey husk enclosing small oil-rich seeds and a mass of glossy fibres known as kapok silk. A single mature tree may produce up to 4,000 fruits in a season.

CEIBA PENTANDRA

Celtis australis
European nettle tree
Verona

In the Sona district of the north Italian city of Verona, at the old settlement of Corte Pietà, you will find what is allegedly the oldest example of *Celtis australis* in Europe. It was planted in around the year 1610, making it more than 400 years old. Currently it stands at approximately 15m/49ft in height, and measures some 6.5m/21ft in circumference. This solitary but impressive tree is an important local landmark, known as the *bagolaro di Sona*. The word *bagolaro* means liar, so the connection is a bit of a mystery, and it actually goes under a wide assortment of local names in Italy. Some other nice examples can be found standing in the ground of the golf club of Verona.

This tree may readily appear to be a splendid contradiction in terms, since it is neither Australian nor is it related to nettles! It is a member of the elm family, also known as the Mediterranean hackberry, the lote or lotus tree and the honeyberry, and the Latin species name appears to refer to the fact that it became extensively naturalised as a weed in New South Wales, where it was first planted as a street tree. Its European range is almost entirely restricted to Italy, although one or two fine veterans have been recorded in France and it was also introduced into England in 1796.

This deciduous tree assumes a fairly even, broadly rounded shape, has a smooth greenish-grey bark and prefers life in dry sandy soils. It is described as a nettle tree purely on account of the shape of its leaves, which are narrow, dark greyish-green above, downy underneath and bear sharp 'teeth' reminiscent of nettles. It flowers in springtime, the flowers containing both male and female parts that are pollinated by bees. The fruits are tiny berries turning from red to dark purple, hanging in short clusters, and the seeds ripen during the autumn. It is fairly frost-resistant and is considered to have good medicinal properties, particularly in the fruits, which are edible and possess a taste similar to that of dates.

In Greek mythology the fruit was supposed to be the lotus of the ancients. When Homer's *Odyssey* describes the 'lotus eaters', it is actually referring to the fruit of this tree.

CELTIS AUSTRALIS

Cercis siliquastrum
Judas tree
Istanbul

Technically, Istanbul is transcontinental, straddling the Bosphorus, the strait that separates Europe from Asia. One of the trees most famously associated with the city is the Judas tree, also known as *erguvan*, a Turkish word that describes the vivid pink colour of the flowers. Judas trees had a special place in Ottoman culture, and they are found growing all along the shores of the Bosphorus, sometimes in dense thickets. Nearly 50,000 *Cercis siliquastrum* have been planted in Istanbul since 2012, designated the year of the *erguvan*, and the tree has been put forward for adoption as the city's official symbol. Festivals are held to celebrate the *erguvan* flowering season in a tradition that goes back to the 15th century.

Indigenous to much of the Mediterranean area, this comparatively small, bushy, deciduous species, rarely extending beyond 10m/33ft in height, borders on being classed as a large shrub. The heart-shaped leaves, about 10cm/4in across, open only after the flowers. The tree comes into bloom during the latter half of April, and is justly famed for its prolific displays of richly pink flowers, each with five petals. These appear in dense clusters on the older trees and are edible. The fruits develop subsequently as flattened, deep-purple-coloured, woody pods that hang down and are about 12cm/5in long. It is, incidentally, from the shape of the fruits that the genus name *Cercis* comes. It is a Greek word meaning a shuttle, and it refers to the resemblance between the seed pods and the age-old device use by weavers.

Cercis siliquastrum is the stuff of legend and poetry. It is one of a number of trees claimed as the gallows on which Judas Iscariot hung himself. As evidence of this shameful association, the tree's branches allegedly drooped, and its once pristine white flowers blushed red. For the Egyptians and Romans, however, the rich colour of its blossom made it a symbol of nobility. A more bizarre legendary claim is that Sultan Süleyman the Magnificent insisted on residing in an *erguvan*-coloured tent during battles.

CERCIS
SILIQUASTRUM

Ceroxylon quindiuense
Wax palm
Bogotá

For about the first 450 years of Bogotá's existence, urban tree plantings largely consisted of exotic species, while native trees were almost wholly ignored. Today that outlook is changing, with the timely realisation that as Colombia's wild areas are being lost, urban refuges are taking on ever-increasing significance for conservation. In 1998, Bogotá's mayor launched a massive tree-planting scheme, with the focus firmly on indigenous flora. From that juncture, iconic species such as the wax palm, Colombia's national tree, became an increasingly common sight in the capital. One of the best places to discover these striking giants is in Independencia Park, stretching from the city's eastern hills down towards Centenario Park. There is also a fine collection in the José Celestino Mutis Botanic Garden, which is dedicated to conserving Colombian plants and is located at Avenue Calle 63.

Ceroxylon quindiuense is a species of palm tree native to the high Andean cloud forests of Colombia and Peru, living at altitudes of up to 3,000m/9,840ft. Slow-growing, with a single trunk, the tree can reach an awesome height of as much as 60m/200ft in the wild – which makes it the world's tallest known monocotyledon. Generally, however, it attains a rather more modest stature. Dark greyish-green pinnate leaves, up to 5m/16ft long and divided into many narrow leaflets, form a distinctive spreading crown. The tree's bark is its most striking feature: smooth, pallid, covered with wax and punctuated by darker leaf scars that form horizontal rings like rungs on a ladder. Inconspicuous male and female flowers bloom on separate trees. The fruits are rounded, up to 2cm/¾in in diameter, forming large orange-red clusters when ripe. Wax palms do not, however, become reproductive for about eighty years.

In the past much damage has been wrought to these remarkable trees through stripping the leaves for the Christian religious celebration of Palm Sunday. Young trees were favoured, being more accessible, and the loss of leaves was often fatal. The trees have also been extensively felled to extract wax for candles, a practice that still continues. The tree is now classed as vulnerable on the IUCN Red List of threatened species and has been legally protected in Colombia since 1985, the year it gained national tree status.

CEROXYLON
QUINDIUENSE

Citrus x *aurantium*
Seville orange
Seville

Seville oranges, it has to be said, are not the sort from which to take a juicy bite. They are bitter! Yet it is easy to be tempted because Seville plays host to anything between 25,000 and 40,000 orange trees, outnumbering any other species in the city. They give the place its identity, and in popular culture, the orange has become emblematic of Seville. Yet neither the tree, nor its blossoms, feature on the city's coat of arms, nor is the species native to Europe. Orange trees are indigenous to southeast Asia, where Chinese tradition claims them to be lucky trees. They found their way initially into the eastern Byzantine wing of the Roman Empire, and from there the Moors introduced them to Spain in the 10th century, doing much to encourage their popularity and planting. Moorish poets were liberal in their praise of the orange tree and its fragrant blossoms.

All oranges cultivated today are actually hybrids of two citrus species. The Seville orange came to the city about 1,000 years ago, and was actively grown from the 12th century onwards, though not for eating. The edible orange *Citrus sinensis*, now planted in commercial orchards, is a sweeter and more palatable choice that was introduced much later than *Citrus* x *aurantium*. These days *Citrus sinensis*, grown in a number of forms and cultivars such as common orange, blood orange, navel orange and clementine, lays claim to being the most cultivated tree worldwide.

The Seville orange tree, like its cousins, is evergreen and provides welcome shade from the sun's heat along the city streets. The trees can live for between 50 and 150 years, growing to a height of 6–8m/20–26ft, depending on the variety, with a fairly low canopy. They thrive best in full sunshine and moist soil, and are not frost-tolerant. The blossoms of *Citrus* x *aurantium*, known locally as *azahar*, are showy and pink or white and at their best in March–early April when urban Seville becomes thoroughly pervaded by their heady aroma. Orange trees can bear fruit during more or less any season of the year.

CITRUS X AURANTIUM

Citrus limon
Lemon tree
Menton

Set between the Mediterranean Sea and mountains, Menton is a town that may not be familiar to everyone, but it can, however, boast rather a lot of lemon trees! It lies in a fairly unique location, shielded from the cold winds coming off the Alps by surrounding hills, which means that it benefits from the warmest winters anywhere in the south of France aside from Corsica. Chiefly for this reason, it is the only town in France where lemons are grown in quantity. Until the 1930s Menton was Europe's main producer of lemons, and today, approximately 5,000 lemon trees, in several varieties, are grown both at Menton and in adjacent communes. Every year, between February and March, the town holds its *Fête du Citron*. This has become the second most important event on the Riviera, after the Nice Carnival, and annually attracts more than 230,000 visitors. During the height of the festivities, giant sculptures built from over 140 tons of lemons and oranges are paraded through the streets on floats, inspired each season by a different theme. At quieter times, you will find interesting citrus collections at the Val Rahmeh Botanic Garden and the Palais de Carnolès, including a lemon cultivar named after the town.

Citrus limon, which may in origin be a hybrid of the lime and the citron, is a small evergreen tree, rarely achieving a height of more than 6m/20ft. The twigs bear stout spines and the ovate leaves, reddish when young, become dark green and leathery. The sweetly scented flowers have five petals, white within and purplish on the outside, surrounding bunches of long stamens with yellow anthers. The familiar yellow fruits range in shape from rounded to oblong, with a blunt, nipple-like extension, and are generally highly acidic (although some varieties have a reduced acid content). The trees are best grown in warm, well-drained soils, sheltered from wind and frost.

Where lemon trees first came from remains a mystery, even though the native range is known to be Asiatic. One possible answer is India and Pakistan, where they are extremely common. Archaeological evidence from Pompeii suggests that lemon trees had reached southern Italy by the 1st century AD, but cultivation did not really get under way until the mid-15th century, in Genoa, merely a short hop along the coast from Menton.

CITRUS LIMON

Cladrastis kentukea
Kentucky yellowwood
Hanover

Occasionally some truly magnificent specimen trees are to be discovered in cities a long way from home. The native range of Kentucky yellowwood, as its name suggests, lies in the southeastern United States, and even there it is quite a rare sight, occurring mainly on limestone cliffs. It grows most commonly along the Kentucky River. So it might seem improbable that a particularly monumental example of the species stands in the Berggarten, just off Herrenhäuser Street, in the German city of Hanover. There are few details available about the age or actual size of this veteran tree, but it is naturally low-branching and sprawls as much as it rises, several of its branches now touching the ground. It is quite an impressive sight! Similar specimen trees of *Cladrastis kentukea* can be found in several other German cities, including Bremen and Potsdam.

In the wild, this deep-rooting deciduous tree can grow, exceptionally, up to 25m/82ft in height. But in cultivation it generally stops at 15m/49ft, with a spread of similar size. The crown is broad and rounded in profile. The trunk will often divide close to the ground, becoming multi-stemmed, and is clothed with smooth, grey bark, in contrast to the reddish-brown of the young twigs. It actually derives its common name from the brilliant yellow colour of the freshly sawn heartwood. The leaves are large, extending to 30cm/12in in length, and are composed of seven to nine broadly ovate leaflets, downy on the underside. In autumn the foliage becomes a delicious blend of gold, yellow and copper tints. In late spring and early summer the tree erupts with masses of fragrant panicles of showy, pendulous cream-coloured flowers, vaguely reminiscent of wisteria. It is reported, however, to flower only periodically in quantity. *Cladrastis* belongs to the bean family and produces flat, green pods, about 12cm/5in long, which become brown as they ripen.

The species suffers from few disease or insect problems, not least because the wood is heavy and hard, which makes it valuable, as and when available, for furniture-making.

CLADRASTIS KENTUKEA

Corymbia ficifolia
Red flowering gum
Perth

Although less common in Perth than the spotted gum, *Corymbia maculata*, this species is prettier to look at. Not a true gum tree but one of three species of 'bloodwood' found in the region, it is about the most spectacular of any of the eucalypts. Within the city confines, among the best places to discover it is on Lord Street in the northeastern suburb of Bassendean. Closer to the city centre it can also be found on Wellington Street in the business district, Jackson Road in the Karawara district, Kent Street, Lansdowne Road in the Kensington district of South Perth, and Lockhart Street close to the Swan River. For golf enthusiasts there is also a brilliant summertime display bordering the ninth and tenth holes of the Lake Karrinyup Country Club course in the north of the city. Kings Park Botanical Garden was once planted with a magnificent avenue of red flowering gum to mark Queen Victoria's jubilee, but sadly most of those trees have since succumbed to disease. *Corymbia ficifolia* is nonetheless strongly recommended by the city authorities for planting both as a street tree and in gardens, because of its masses of colourful flowers, and its urban population is increasing.

The natural range of the species is limited to a very small coastal area of open forest east of Walpole, and about 400km/250mi southeast of Perth. It is a fairly fast-growing tree that typically reaches a height of about 10m/33ft, occasionally more, with a broad-spreading canopy that can become fairly straggly. The limbs are clothed with a rough, brownish-grey furrowed bark that, unlike some other eucalypts, is not discarded annually. The evergreen leaves are thick, darkish blue-green and faintly aromatic. This species is also quirky in that it only puts on growth in spring. This means that it does not obscure the flowers, which are the crowning glory of the tree. They erupt in large clusters or corymbs towards the end of the branches in late summer, and thus they make a very prominent spectacle. Generally a brilliant red colour, they can also appear in different shades ranging from cream through pink to deep crimson. The flowers are fertilised by bees and butterflies, and the resultant fruit is a woody flask-shaped nut.

Until 1995, the species was known as *Eucalyptus ficifolia*, after which the 'bloodwood' species and some others, including lemon-scented gum and spotted gum, were placed in the new genus, *Corymbia*.

CORYMBIA FICIFOLIA

Delonix regia
Flame tree
Hong Kong

Hong Kong is rather a long way from the native home of *Delonix regia* in northern and western Madagascar, where it is now under severe threat in what remains of the dry, deciduous forests. This is surely one of the most gloriously eye-catching floral trees, grown these days as a popular ornamental throughout much of the tropics. Although it was widely cultivated from the 19th century onwards, the original Malagasy source of the flame tree had for a long time been lost to science, and was only rediscovered in the 1930s.

It was introduced to Hong Kong in the early 1900s, and by the late 1920s hundreds had been planted across the city and the New Territories. Flame trees have since also become popular in southern China. In Hong Kong, the responsibility for planting and maintaining the trees today rests with various landscape management companies, and in the city's parks and gardens it still seems to thrive in a modern, densely populated and 'vertically urban' environment. It is worth visiting the Repulse Bay area, or a central location like Victoria Park, to see its colours at their best. However, it does not cope well with the hazards of pavement life, because it is not tolerant of traffic fumes, malnutrition or frost, and it is also prone to root rot. For these reasons the Hong Kong government no longer supports planting it in crowded urban areas.

The flame tree is not especially tall, growing little higher than 15m/49ft. It tends to spread horizontally, forming an umbrella-shaped canopy with a width of 15m/49ft or more, and also demands space for an equally spreading root system. It is deciduous in regions with a marked dry season, but otherwise keeps its ferny foliage all year. The beauty of the tree rests in its masses of flame-red flowers, which erupt throughout May and June in such quantities that they virtually obscure the greenery. Each flower expands to about 12cm/5in and is formed of five spoon-shaped petals. The flowers last for weeks, but are produced in such profusion that when they fall they create constant work for gardeners and park cleaners. The long, blackening pods are characteristic of the bean family, to which the tree belongs.

DELONIX REGIA

Eucalyptus camaldulensis
Red river gum
Melbourne

In Melbourne, where more than 82,000 trees populate the roadsides and parks, gum trees outnumber any other group by far. Finding them is easy. The tricky part probably lies in telling them apart, as there are several species present. For red river gum, look no further than Smithfield Road, where a double avenue of trees borders the southeastern perimeter of Flemington Racecourse. There is also a large number dotted around Riverside Park, at the southwest end of Smithfield Road, and the species dominates parts of J.J. Holland Park, a few blocks to the east. Another splendid avenue lines the Royal Park side of Gatehouse Street, with a profusion of the trees scattered throughout the park itself. More can be discovered adjacent to Elliott Avenue, the road dividing Royal Park from Melbourne Zoo.

Eucalyptus camaldulensis is a true gum tree, with the widest distribution of any eucalypt on the continent, and to many Australians it will be both familiar and iconic. In the wild it tends to grow alongside inland rivers, where it dominates the landscape and often serves to stabilise riverbanks against erosion. This tall evergreen tree can reach 45m/148ft in height, offering welcome shade when temperatures soar in central Australia. Its sturdy trunk is clothed in smooth, whitish-grey bark with patches of reddish-brown, which peels off periodically in long ribbon-like flakes. The mature leaves are lance-shaped, broadly tapering and dull blue-green, containing obvious oil glands. Flowers emerge in summer, held in stalked clusters. The buds are at first protected by a curious little cap called an operculum; this falls away to reveal a mass of white stamens, but no visible petals. The fruit is hemispherical and contains yellowish-brown seeds.

The tree has gained the morbid tag of 'widow-maker' because of a tendency to shed fairly massive boughs without warning. This is largely due to the brittleness of the wood, though some authorities consider it to be a method of self-pruning to conserve water. The 'red' in its common name derives from the colour of the wood, which ranges from brilliant red to almost black.

EUCALYPTUS
CAMALDULENSIS

Fagus sylvatica
European beech
Utrecht

One might justly claim that these glorious trees are to be found gracing the confines of most European cities, but if you are a visitor to the Dutch city of Utrecht, there are some particularly striking examples of European beech to be discovered in Juliana Park, created by a city benefactor in 1903. The pretty copper beech at the corner of Zonnenburg and Lepelenburg was planted in 1945 to commemorate the liberation of Utrecht. The city also has its share of monumental trees. Near Emmalaan roundabout stands a massive copper beech planted in 1888 that now stands just short of 22m/72ft, with a girth of nearly 4m/13ft. To the northwest of the city, in the park of De Haar Castle, there is an even grander specimen planted in about 1850, rising to 33m/105ft with a girth of nearly 6m/20ft. It is well worth making a trip out to the Op Hees Nature Reserve, situated northeast of the city, where you can wander along a splendid beech-framed walkway.

Fagus sylvatica is a slow-growing tree with a lifespan of about 200 years – although some veterans see out as many as 300 years – and can eventually achieve a considerable height of as much as 45m/148ft. It rises up on a sturdy trunk clothed in smooth, light grey bark. Given space, the branches form a broad, elegant crown. If beech trees have a built-in weakness it lies in their stability. The root system is particularly shallow and does not anchor the tree well, which makes it particularly prone to toppling over in strong winds. The danger is exacerbated in summer because the leaf canopy is dense. This also tends to exclude light from the woodland floor beneath the beech trees, which is characteristically bare of other vegetation. The oval leaves have a pleated look. Young leaves are pale green and downy, later becoming darker and glossy; in autumn the foliage turns a glorious gold. European beech does not flower until it is at least thirty years old, after which it produces tiny male and female wind-pollinated catkins, borne on the same tree. Nuts form within a bristly husk that opens in autumn, allowing the mature seeds to fall to the ground as 'beechmast'.

FAGUS SYLVATICA

Ficus benghalensis
Banyan
Howrah

One cannot travel very far in India without encountering a banyan tree, considered to be sacred and India's national tree. Howrah, located on the west bank of the Hooghly River, and essentially industrial in character, is the second largest city in Bengal after Kolkata. Extending inland from the riverside lies the Acharya Jagadish Chandra Bose Indian Botanic Garden, renowned not least for one extraordinary resident: the Great Banyan. Although its exact age is unclear, the tree is known to be more than 250 years old, as several 19th-century travel guides reveal it was a spectacular sight even then. The tree survived two cyclones in the 1860s, but when it became diseased in the 1920s the main trunk was removed. This left a clonal colony of vast dimensions that has now taken on the appearance of a minor forest. While not quite the world's biggest banyan, it comes close, with some jaw-dropping statistics. The canopy has a circumference of 486m/1,594ft. Parts of it reach a height of almost 25m/82ft. As in other figs, *Ficus benghalensis* develops aerial roots, and it has been calculated that the Great Banyan of Howrah currently boasts 3,772 of them.

Like other 'strangler figs', it starts life as an epiphyte growing on a host tree, which it eventually suffocates. The species is indigenous to tropical forests in the Indian subcontinent, and is the largest in the world in terms of the spread of the canopy, which makes it a popular shade tree. The banyan is supported on a massive, fluted main trunk with smooth, greyish bark. The combined circle of trunks developed from the aerial roots of an original tree can reach colossal dimensions of about 200m/656ft. Its leathery, broadly ovate leaves, up to 20cm/8in long, have pronounced veins. Male and female flowers are inconspicuous, borne on the same tree in the leaf axils, and after fertilisation the fruits have a typical fig-like appearance, pinkish-red when ripe, but are not especially palatable.

In common with the related species *Ficus religiosa*, the banyan is reputed to have been linked with the enlightenment of at least one of the subsequent incarnations of the Buddha, and is said to represent eternal life. The resin of the tree is used in the production of shellac or French polish.

FICUS BENGHALENSIS

Ficus macrophylla
Moreton Bay fig
Sydney

This is surely one of the most frequently encountered trees in Sydney's streetscape. Not to be confused with Hill's weeping fig, also common in the city, Moreton Bay fig is an outstanding species for its sheer presence. Arcadia Road, in the heart of the Glebe district, has a spectacular avenue of these fine trees. More than forty are also planted in a double row along Bridge Road, which runs between the Sydney Fish Market and the City Quarter. There is a large mature specimen overshadowing St Saviour's Anglican church in Redfern, and others in the grounds of the Merewether Building of Sydney University. A particularly impressive veteran can be found in adjacent Butlin Avenue, and two more, probably planted in the late 1920s, stand together on the corner of Catherine Street and Mount Vernon Street, just north of the university campus. Redfern Park and Waterloo Park also hold some notable examples. In short, you are spoilt for choice.

Ficus macrophylla is a large evergreen banyan tree reaching a height of 60m/200ft in the wild. Its natural range extends down a large part of Australia's eastern seaboard. Much of its allure rests in the massively buttressed trunk base festooned with aerial or prop roots, resulting in a 'melting' appearance. It is among the so-called strangler figs, adapted for life in forests where there is intense competition for light. The seedlings germinate in crevices high in the canopy of other trees, beginning life as epiphytes. They then grow roots downward, eventually suffocating the host and becoming freestanding trees in their own right. Mature trees are clothed with rough bark. The leathery, elliptical leaves are dark green and glossy above and rust-coloured beneath. All parts exude a milky sap when damaged. The flowers are hidden on the inside of the immature fruit and can only be pollinated by a particular wasp, which, in turn, relies on this fig species to complete its life cycle. The figs become purplish on ripening, and can be produced more or less year-round, but don't be tempted to eat them as they are dry and not particularly palatable.

FICUS MACROPHYLLA

Ficus religiosa
Bodhi tree
Rangoon

The People's Square and Park, which once lay within the grounds of Queen Shin Sawbu's palace, cover about 28 hectares/69 acres and contain seventy-two tree species. Among the most celebrated of these is a magnificent *Ficus religiosa*, the sacred tree beneath one of which Gautama Buddha attained enlightenment more than 2,500 years ago. By any standards this is an impressive specimen, standing on the upper terrace of the famous Shwedagon Pagoda, which in turn occupies a high point in the landscape. Surrounded by a raised plinth, and accompanied by a small shrine, it is locally reputed to have begun life as a seedling of the original bodhi tree, which grew in Bihar, India, but in reality it is anything from 100 to 150 years old and is very unlikely to be a descendant of the original.

Belonging to the mulberry family, *Ficus religiosa* is indigenous to India and Indochina. Semi-evergreen in monsoon regions, it reaches a height of about 30m/100ft, with a trunk often buttressed at the base and as much as 3m/10ft in diameter. In common with other 'strangler' figs, it can initially grow as an epiphyte by germinating from a seed deposited on the upper branches of a host tree, which it then progressively outcompetes by putting down long aerial roots. Once mature, it possesses a fairly wide-spreading canopy clothed with heart-shaped, strongly veined leaves that extend into distinctively pointed tips. The leaves are held on long, slender stalks. Like other figs, this species relies on a specific wasp to reproduce. The insect lays its eggs in the tiny female flowers and in doing so deposits pollen brought from other trees. The small figs are edible but not especially pleasant.

At Monywa, you can take a trip to the Bodhi Tahtaung Pagoda and there contemplate a striking vista of a thousand *Ficus religiosa* trees that were planted during the 1960s. In carefully regimented rows, each has its own attendant Buddha statue. The plantation is overshadowed by a colossal reclining Buddha occupying an adjoining hillside.

FICUS RELIGIOSA

Fraxinus uhdei
Shamel ash
Mexico City

Better known in Mexico City by its Spanish name *fresno*, this ash tops the list as the most frequently planted tree of the city's streets. *Fraxinus uhdei* is an attractive ornamental with the advantage of being both fast-growing and tolerant of air pollution, an essential requirement for any plant attempting to thrive in a city surrounded by mountains that make it difficult for the notorious traffic fumes to escape. Not only a good provider of shade along urban walkways, in itself it is also shade-tolerant, so it will thrive in the permanent shadow of tall buildings. It frequently towers over plazas and walkways, and often seems to be emerging untroubled from concrete pavements. Away from the busy streets, there are some fine specimens to be seen in the Bosque de Chapultepec, in the western part of the city. Another pleasant and comparatively peaceful location holding big shamel ashes is the botanic garden of the Institute of Biology, off Avenida Insurgentes Sur in the south of the city.

The native range of *Fraxinus uhdei* extends from the mountainous canyons of south-central Mexico, which lie just to the north of Mexico City, southwards into areas of Central America. It is a largely evergreen member of the olive family, with only periodic leaf fall. The tree can grow vigorously to a height of 35m/115ft. Its canopy is at first fairly narrow and upright, but at maturity may achieve a spread of 30m/100ft. The trunk is smooth-barked when young, becoming slightly roughened. The pinnate leaves are composed of seven to nine sharply pointed, ovate leaflets with serrated margins. Inconspicuous male and female flowers are borne on separate trees in midwinter, just before the appearance of any new leaves. Winged seeds are produced in copious quantities.

The tree is not without its health problems. In Mexico City it has been found to be particularly susceptible to infection with the plant parasite, mistletoe. The species has also suffered decline in recent times through the ravages of a bark-boring beetle.

FRAXINUS UHDEI

Ginkgo biloba
Maidenhair tree
Tokyo

To discover a remarkable species that to all intents and purposes is a living fossil, one could do worse than visit the city of Tokyo and seek out its famous ginkgo trees. One of the most celebrated places to admire these beautiful prehistoric forms is the Icho Namiki, running through Meiji Jingu Gaien Park in central Tokyo. The 146 trees that make up the avenue do not reflect their natural shape, however, because they have been trimmed to look like tall spires. Green in summer, by late autumn the foliage has turned a glorious hue, and in November the passer-by walks beneath a magical golden tunnel. A second Tokyo venue well worth visiting for its formally shaped ginkgos is the Showa Memorial Park, in the western part of the city. To find ginkgo looking more as nature intended, try the southern side of Yoyogi Koen Park where, with the maples, they provide a colourful autumnal mix of gold and red. The Imperial Palace East Garden also has several mature ginkgos. The oldest ginkgo in the city, a male tree allegedly planted some 1,200 years ago, stands by the Zenpuku-ji Buddhist temple in Azabu district.

In a natural setting, the trees reach up to 50m/164ft in height, though in cultivation they are generally smaller. The roots can penetrate deeply, as far as 10m/33ft. Renowned for their longevity, evidence of the ginkgo's prehistoric ancestors has been discovered in fossils dating back 270 million years, and they are thought to provide an evolutionary link between ferns and flowering plants. They were perhaps among the first trees to populate the earth with leafy structures, but although they bear distinctive fan-shaped foliage, divided into two lobes, hence the name *biloba*, these leaves are far removed from those one finds on a modern flowering plant.

Sometimes known in Japan as an 'upside down tree', this quaint name derives from the way that the branches, when left to their own devices, grow downward, and very old trees can develop limbs that become aerial roots or so-called stalactite branches.

GINKGO BILOBA

Gleditsia triacanthos
Honey locust
Toronto

Toronto is a city of more than ten million trees, of which about three and a half million adorn public parks, another half a million stand as street trees and the rest grow on private property. Indigenous to the east-central United States and Ontario, but comparatively rare in the wild in Canada, *Gleditsia triacanthos* was probably planted by early settlers to attract honeybees. It has become increasingly popular in Toronto, particularly in the newer neighbourhoods, and is considered one of the finest shade trees for the city. Honey locusts grow along Bay Street, which runs north from the bay area, and in St Joseph Street and Wellesley Street, both leading from Queen's Park. Two nice examples await discovery at the northern end of Queen's Park itself. Other single trees are located in the Trinity Bellwoods Park (in the section adjacent to Queen Street West) and in Orchard Park, by Dundas Street East – not forgetting Toronto Island Park, reached by the Centre Island ferry.

The species can grow to a height of about 30m/100ft, with a broad, flattish-topped crown. It is both hardy and drought-resistant, and is fairly tolerant of urban conditions including soil compaction and salt pollution. But it is reasonably short-lived, rarely surviving for more than 120 years, and the limbs also tend to be brittle. It is deciduous, and when the boughs are devoid of leaves in winter, the tree often reveals a distinctively angular appearance. The bark in young growth is smooth, but with age develops furrows and ridges. The cultivated variety also lacks the three-pronged, reddish thorns that are found on the trunks of wild trees, a characteristic which probably arose as a defence against browsing animals. The leaves of mature trees are pinnate, with rows of small green leaflets about 2.5cm/1in long, turning yellow in autumn. Clusters of strongly scented, tiny flowers emerge from the leaf axils in late spring. The fruit is a typical legume 'bean pod' that ripens in early autumn.

The common name, 'honey locust', remains tantalisingly obscure, but clearly had some significance, now lost, either for the First Nations tribes or early Canadian colonists.

GLEDITSIA
TRIACANTHOS

Handroanthus chrysotrichus
Golden trumpet tree
Rio de Janeiro

Formerly named *Tabebuia chrysotricha* but reclassified botanically in 2007, this spectacular flowering species is indigenous to southern and eastern Brazil, where it grows naturally in most of the states, and to parts of Argentina. It is Brazil's national tree and is widely planted in towns and cities as a showy ornamental. Rio de Janeiro's botanic garden holds some fine specimens. The tree copes well with life in full sun and is fairly drought-tolerant, but it needs a regular water supply during the summer months, and does best when growing in consistently moist soil. It is thus well suited to Rio's humid climate.

A member of the tropical *Bignonia* family, which contains some of the world's most ostentatious trees, including, most notably, jacarandas. The golden trumpet is fast-growing and reaches 12m/39ft in height, occasionally more, on a sturdy trunk clothed in hard, fissured bark. The palmate leaves, each with five to seven dark greyish-green leaflets, have a soft, velvety texture to the touch, and are covered with rusty brown hairs. Bright yellow, sometimes reddish-tinted, flowers erupt between late winter and mid-spring, generally when the trees are devoid of leaves, which permits them to be extremely showy. The tubular flowers with five lobes are held in big rounded clusters that look not unlike rhododendron blossom. They produce copious nectar, making them attractive to bees and some species of hummingbird. The fruit is a long, velvety, pale brown pod that overwinters on the branches.

The tree is valued locally for medicinal uses, the bark being incorporated into a number of preparations. However, parts of the plant are known to cause allergic reactions when handled. The wood is extremely hard, and of dense, fine-grained quality, so is particularly sought-after for furniture-making. These days the popularity of the species as a shady garden tree, and for planting on roadsides, has extended beyond Brazil, and it is now a common sight in California. There are also increasing concerns that it risks becoming an invasive species in parts of subtropical Australia.

HANDROANTHUS
CHRYSOTRICHUS

Jacaranda mimosifolia
Jacaranda
Lisbon

One does not need to travel very far through the streets of Lisbon, during spring or early summer, before the senses are assaulted by the delightful fragrance and colours of the blue jacaranda tree, which in Portugal is pronounced 'zacaranda'. The main streets are planted with nearly 2,000 jacarandas, which normally bloom and are at their showiest in May. It remains a mystery as to when and how the species was first introduced here, but suffice to say that the trees have become known as a part of Lisbon's identity. Some of the best places to see them en masse include the Avenue 5 de Outubro, Avenue Dom Carlos I, Eduardo VII Park, and Largo do Carmo. They can look equally stunning as specimen trees on their own, but when they are lining either side of Lisbon's main avenues the panorama in full bloom can be traffic-stopping.

Native to extensive subtropical swathes of South and Central America, the glorious appearance of the tree in flower has made it a firm favourite in all parts of the world where there is a suitable climate, and these days it is grown as far away as Nepal. It is naturally a fast-growing species, thriving in sandy soils with good drainage and plenty of sunshine. If grown from seed, the tree can take up to fourteen years before it blooms, eventually reaching a height of about 15m/49ft. The jacaranda has spreading branches that arise from a short, often distorted trunk with a typically scaly bark. Although evergreen in warm and wet climes, in other regions the fern-like bipinnate leaves fall in winter or during dry periods. The violet-blue, trumpet-shaped flowers are tightly packed into flowerheads known as panicles. Each flower consists of five petals joined to form a tube, not unlike a foxglove. The flowering period lasts for up to two months, with blooms appearing in successive waves. The fruit is a woody pod which, when ripe, releases little winged seeds that are transported on air currents.

One of the clear advantages of planting jacaranda as a street tree, aside from its prolific flowering, is that its roots penetrate downward, and so tend not to damage pavements and tarmac. The jacaranda, however, is tragically under threat from unregulated commercial exploitation, as its fine timber is increasingly in demand both for furniture-making and for the fashioning of musical instruments.

JACARANDA MIMOSIFOLIA

Juglans mandshurica
Manchurian walnut
Riga

Although from its name it is one of the more improbable trees to discover in the Baltic city of Riga, the Manchurian walnut was introduced to the wider Russian Empire by German landscape architect Georg Kuphaldt, who became Riga's first director of parks and gardens in 1880. This was one of a variety of trees he planted along the canal running through the city, a green space known today as the canal garden. Kuphaldt planted others of the species in the Vērmanes Garden, the oldest public park in the city, located close by the Brīvības bulvāris; this boulevard is also the place to see a monumental, multi-stemmed Manchurian walnut almost 5m/16ft in girth. An intriguing specimen with tentacle-like branches lying prone on the ground grows in parkland by the Kemeri Sanatorium, about an hour out of town.

Juglans mandshurica is a deciduous tree from mixed forests at altitudes of up to 2,800m/9,186ft, meaning it is extremely hardy, tolerating temperatures as low as minus 45°C. The hostile environments in which it is often found in the wild are characterised by a short growing season, and to compensate for this the rate of growth is particularly rapid. In the wild it can reach a height of about 25m/82ft, with rough, fissured bark when mature and upright branches. The remarkably large pinnate leaves, up to 90cm/35in long, consist of seven to nineteen broad leaflets. Long male catkins develop in spring, followed by the female flowers, which are arranged in spikes and are wind-pollinated. These ripen into familiar thick-shelled walnuts during late summer and early autumn, each protected by an elongated, velvety green husk.

Grown as an ornamental across much of the northern hemisphere, but more often seen in the colder regions, Manchurian walnut is especially admired for the exotic look of its foliage. In Riga the tree has recently been selected for inclusion in parkland designed to surround a major new residential scheme called Ezerparks. The city is proud of its green spaces: a specially commissioned bench commemorating Kuphaldt's contribution can be found in the canal gardens.

JUGLANS
MANDSHURICA

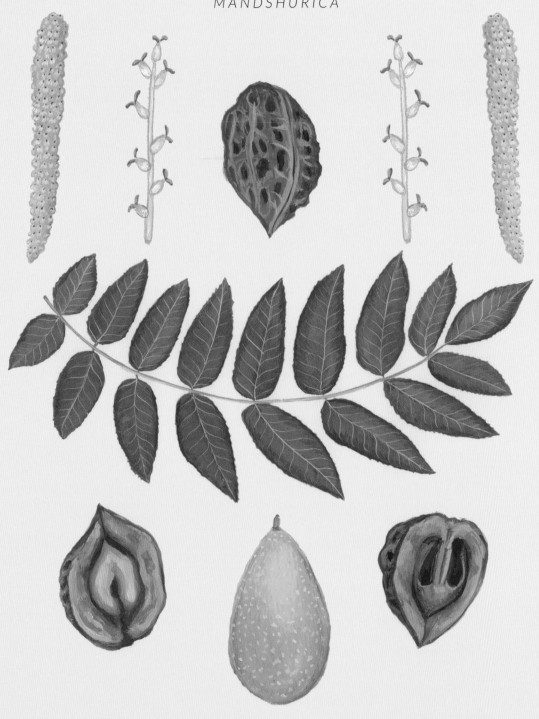

Liriodendron tulipifera
Tulip tree
Lexington

In 1956 the State of Kentucky adopted the tulip tree as an official emblem, and it remains thus – although the accolade has been lost in favour of a rival, the Kentucky coffee tree. *Liriodendron tulipifera* is one of the tallest native American hardwoods, as well as a popular ornamental for larger spaces and an approved street tree in Lexington. Some particularly fine specimens can be discovered in the State Botanical Garden's arboretum on the campus of Kentucky University, located off Alumni Drive. Beaver Creek Wilderness in Floyd County, is home to the most impressive living veteran of the species in the state, which is nearing 50m/164ft in height. Other fine examples grow in the Mammoth Cave National Park, southwest of Lexington.

Also known misleadingly as the tulip poplar, since it is actually a member of the magnolia family, the tree is native to eastern North America, where it thrives in moist soils along stream banks, often in mountainous areas. It possesses many of the ingredients that make certain species popular for urban planting – it is fast-growing, low-maintenance and the canopy provides good shade cover. It prefers full sun but is only moderately drought-tolerant; dry conditions can result in early leaf fall. The species grows with a straight, stout trunk clothed in furrowed grey bark. The leaves are yellow on emerging, becoming green with age and then developing a fine golden colouring in autumn. As its name suggests, the tulip tree bears beautiful cup-shaped flowers that erupt into blossom in May and June, often high up in the canopy. The orange and pale green flowers are rich in nectar, and thus a favourite of bees and hummingbirds. The petals fall fairly quickly, leaving behind cone-shaped clusters of winged seeds that are dispersed when ripe in the autumn.

In days gone by, legendary frontiersman Daniel Boone claimed that the trunks of tulip trees made the best dugout canoes. The logs were once used for cabins, railway sleepers and pipelines. In the Lexington of today, some older houses still have floors crafted from tulip tree wood.

LIRIODENDRON
TULIPIFERA

Litchi chinensis
Lychee
Singapore

To discover one of the grandest of these iconic trees, the visitor to Singapore could do worse than aim for Mount Rosie Road, formerly a private driveway to some elegant bungalows, and locate lamp post LP12 (yes, they are numbered!). Here they will find what is probably the largest roadside specimen of *Litchi chinensis*, a heritage tree standing at an impressive 18m/59ft tall, with a girth of more than 8m/26ft. In a more tranquil setting, the Singapore Botanic Gardens, set up on Government Hill by Sir Stamford Raffles in 1822 and now a UNESCO World Heritage Site, is also well stocked with lychee trees.

Indigenous to the Guangdong and Fujian provinces of southern China, *Litchi chinensis* was first recorded in cultivation in AD 1059. Over the centuries, on account of the popularity of its sweet fruit, the plant has been spread through cultivation into southeast Asia and India. It thrives anywhere that conditions are warm and humid in summer with high rainfall, though it also benefits from a cool dry spell before flowering. Related to the rambutan and longan trees, this slow-growing, evergreen tree can reach 30m/100ft in height but rarely surpasses 15m/49ft. The dense, rounded canopy, atop a short, stocky trunk, is composed of glossy, leathery pinnate leaves. These are divided into four to eight leaflets, bronze at first but becoming dark green. The leaves are designed to repel water and are known as laurophyllic. Small yellowish-green apetalous flowers, sometimes with purple tints, appear in spring in bunches at the tips of the branches. The fruits develop subsequently in hanging clusters of between two and thirty. Each is rounded, about 3cm/1¼in in diameter, and protected by a thin, pinkish-red leathery skin. The fruit is fragrant, particularly juicy and sweet, containing a hard, oblong seed surrounded by an aril that is a translucent pinkish-white colour.

The plant has long been used in traditional medicine, and the seeds when powdered provide an effective analgesic. By repute, the fruit was in heavy demand by the favourite concubine of Emperor Li Longji. Such is the power of love that he was obliged to have it delivered to the capital, on a regular basis, at considerable expense.

LITCHI CHINENSIS

Magnolia grandiflora
Laurel magnolia
Valencia

When visiting the city of Valencia, one of the places to admire magnolias at their showy best is the park named El Parterre, near the Centro Cultural de los Ejércitos. Laid out in the mid-19th century, this ornamental garden plays host to a riot of *Magnolia grandiflora* mingling with palms and pines. Nearly fifty veteran magnolias were planted here more than a hundred years ago, and today four very large specimen trees remain, their branches spread so low that they almost touch the ground. A short distance away is a small park, La Glorieta, which is also well stocked with these magnificent trees, some known to be more than 200 years old. Another charming spot for spectacular specimen magnolias is the neoclassical Alameda Park, created in the 17th century.

Most species grow to over 15m/49ft tall, although the main trunk tends to be quite short. Some veteran trees possess extraordinary twisted and exposed root systems. The trees are evergreen, with leaves that are large, between 10–20cm/4–8in long, glossy dark green above and often rust-coloured beneath. The magnolias of Valencia are in bloom from mid-May to July, and the flowers are unusual in that instead of true petals and sepals, the flowers are built of tough, waxy lobes called carpals or *tépalos*. They are pollinated by beetles, which populated the earth long before bees appeared, and the robustness of the flowers is a survival adaptation to prevent beetle damage. The fruit looks like a small pineapple, made up of individual follicles that separate when ripe, and fall to earth leaving a persistent central core perched on the branch.

Named after Pierre Magnol, a celebrated French botanist who died in 1715, the genus *Magnolia* is of very ancient origin, thought in evolutionary terms to be some twenty million years old. Many of the 120 known species originate from southeast Asia, but the laurel magnolias that predominate in Valencia were imported originally into Spain from North America, where they are native to several southeastern states. The trees have flourished in Valencia's warm, rich soil, where they provide welcome shade from the summer heat.

MAGNOLIA
GRANDIFLORA

Malus baccata
Siberian crab apple
Moscow

In the chilly climes of northern Europe only a limited number of trees bear blossom, one of which is *Malus baccata*. It manages to cope with the cool summers, low light levels and severe winter temperatures that are familiar in high-latitude cities like Moscow. The city has recently adopted a one-million tree-planting programme, with the Siberian crab apple and cultivars such as 'Street Parade' among the trees officially recommended. The selection of this species has been made not merely because of its winter-hardy quality: it has the added advantage of being low-maintenance and ideally suited where there is insufficient space for a larger tree. Sixteen Moscow streets were originally selected for the programme, and Siberian crab apple is one of four species that can be found, for example, planted along Voznesensky Pereulok.

Indigenous to much of northern Asia, from Russia to Korea, and at higher elevations extending its range as far south as Nepal, the tree is also known as the Manchurian or Chinese crab apple. Belonging to the *Malus* genus, it is among the tallest and most resistant to frost and pest damage. Favouring well-drained, fairly acid soils, mature trees can achieve a height of 14m/46ft with a rounded canopy of downwardly arching branches bearing reddish-brown young twigs. Roughened, scaly greyish bark clothes the trunk. The deciduous green leaves are elliptical in shape with pointed tips. The tree bears fragrant white blossoms grouped in showy clusters or umbels which, in Moscow, appear in late spring, and the small, edible crab apples, each about the size of a cherry, mature in early autumn, often persisting on the tree for some time.

Moscow has evolved comparatively recently as a green city, though not always successfully. Street trees were first planted in the 1930s under the instruction of Stalin, who concluded that the concrete jungle he had created needed freshening up. But there was little thought to the needs of the trees, resulting in the planting of many female poplars that each spring discharged large numbers of fluffy seeds, known as *pukh*, bringing frustration to the trees and misery to asthma sufferers. Most of these trees are now being progressively removed and replaced with more appropriate species, including crab apple, maple and rowan.

MALUS BACCATA

Melaleuca citrina
Lemon bottlebrush
San Francisco

Lemon bottlebrush does not refer to the flowers, but to the lemony scent of the leaves when crushed. Although this is not the commonest of trees in central San Francisco, it is nonetheless hardly possible to tread the sidewalks of the city for any distance before encountering one. Technically a large flowering shrub, it is on the official list of trees approved for street planting, and it is certainly one of the prettier species. To discover one of the most notable specimens, head out to Pacific Avenue. At 909 Montgomery Street there stands a fine example, and a short distance away there are two large weeping *Melaleuca viminalis*. Another lemon bottlebrush worth seeking out stands on Potrero Hill, on the east side of 400 block in Arkansas Street. Fine examples can also be found in Golden Gate Park. The tree is, however, not native to North America and is in fact indigenous to Australia. It is widely cultivated in many parts of the world, including Europe, and in some areas it has become naturalised.

The lemon bottlebrush is hardy for urban areas as it is tolerant of air pollution, fairly resistant to disease and not particularly large, making it useful for relatively cramped urban spaces, especially where overhead wires are potentially a problem. It typically grows to a height of 8–10m/26–33ft, with a spread of about 5m/16ft, forming a densely rounded, evergreen canopy. The narrowly ovate leaves are copper-coloured when young, later turning green. The flowers, blooming from late winter onwards and appearing in successive waves, are large and showy, consisting of dense clusters of long, bright red stamens that bunch together in a cylindrical shape resembling a traditional bottlebrush. The petals are inconspicuous. The flowers produce copious nectar, attracting hummingbirds (but also making the ground sticky underfoot when they fall). The fruit is a woody capsule that can persist for some years on the branch.

The scientific name *Melaleuca citrina* is not yet accepted by all authorities, and the tree is often encountered in books under a previous scientific name, *Callistemon citrinus*. *Callistemon* derives from two Greek words meaning beautiful and stamen, and perhaps better sums up the floral appeal of this delightful tree.

MELALEUCA CITRINA

Melaleuca quinquenervia
Broad-leaved paperbark
Brisbane

Also known in Australia as 'teatree', broad-leaved paperbark constitutes an important part of the Brisbane city council's street tree planting programme. Some of the more striking specimen trees can be discovered in the northern suburb of Bracken Ridge and in adjoining Carseldine, a little further to the southwest. Directly across the river from the business district there are some more good examples in Kangaroo Point. They are also to be seen in Bridgeman Downs, Whites Hill, Fortitude Valley, Acacia Ridge, Ballymore, Carina Heights and, south of the city, in Berrinba.

A member of the myrtle family, the native range of *Melaleuca quinquenervia* extends down the coast of eastern Australia between Cape York and Botany Bay. It is also found on the islands of New Caledonia and Papua New Guinea. In its native environment, it grows near to watercourses, estuaries and swamps where groundwater is close to the surface. The tree can live for over 100 years, and has become popular with the authorities for urban planting on roadsides because it grows typically to about 20m/66ft in height, sometimes more, but its canopy only extends to about 10m/33ft in width, providing shade without being a significant traffic hazard. In Brisbane, however, planting is only permitted on wide footpaths. It is also hardy and will tolerate poor drainage. It earns its name 'paperbark' due to the characteristic annual shedding of multiple bark layers in thick, white papery strips, so that the tree trunk takes on a permanently untidy but charming appearance. It bears large, leathery, greyish-green lance-shaped leaves (which are sought-after by koalas) that can be up to 7cm/2¾in long, and the name *quinquenervia* refers to five prominent veins that run down the leaf like nerves. Between September and March, flowers are produced at the ends of the branches, in the form of little 'bottlebrush' spikes with small insignificant petals surrounding bundles of white or cream-coloured stamens.

The tree has been extensively introduced through the tropics as an ornamental, although it sheds considerable amounts of seed and can rapidly become an invasive problem. One unique place in Australia where you can discover the trees planted as a complete avenue is Sydney's Centennial Parklands.

MELALEUCA
QUINQUENERVIA

Metasequoia glyptostroboides
Dawn redwood
Strasbourg

This, by any standards, is an impressive tree. In Strasbourg one of the more monumental living European specimens stands in the Jardin Botanique: planted in 1955, it is now just over 60 years old. Also known as the Chinese Szechuan fir, the species is fairly unusual in that it is one of the deciduous conifers, shedding its leaves in autumn. The dawn redwood has a curious history: its ancestors populated the earth as far back in time as 100 million years ago, during the Late Cretaceous period, and were thought to have become extinct by the Pleistocene (1.6 million years ago). But in 1941, at the time of the Chinese revolution, a number of living examples that appear more or less morphologically identical to the fossil records were discovered by a Japanese palaeontologist in the province of Szechuan. Today the area has been thoroughly surveyed and it is known that about 6,000 dawn redwood trees survive there. The first French specimen was planted in the Alpine Garden of the Museum of Natural History in Paris in 1948.

The tree favours wet, acidic, sandy soils, and its rate of growth is very rapid. It has been suggested the dawn redwood could have a lifespan of at least 300 years. Conical in profile, the branches are carried up on a straight trunk, which becomes distinctively widened at the base. The surface layer of bark is grey in colour but where it breaks away, in characteristically thin strips, it reveals an orange under-surface. The soft, bright green leaflets eventually take on a rich, copper-red hue in autumn. Small male and female cones are borne separately on the same tree. The yellow males are held in pendant clusters, while the females ripen from green to brown, eventually releasing winged seeds. The fruits are cone-shaped, small, green, scaly and borne on long stalks; the species name *glyptostroboides* refers to their 'sculptured' appearance.

The popular name 'dawn redwood' refers in part to the colour of the wood, while the dawn epithet probably derives from its 'rebirth' each springtime. The species is classed as endangered on the IUCN Red List.

METASEQUOIA
GLYPTOSTROBOIDES

Metrosideros excelsa
Pohutukawa
Wellington

This is the New Zealand Christmas tree, whose Maori name is *rata*, producing a brilliant floral display, most commonly of crimson flowers, between November and January. The species can be found in many coastal areas of New Zealand, but it is a common sight planted around the streets of Wellington, at the southern end of the North Island. Heritage specimens can be discovered in Aparima Avenue, Britomart Street, Chelmsford Street and Holloway Road. They can also be admired around the harbour area, and along the coastline as far as Scorching Bay.

Belonging to the myrtle family, *Metrosideros excelsa* is an evergreen tree growing to a height of 25m/82ft, with a broadly spreading canopy, borne up on multiple trunks adorned with fibrous, matted aerial roots. It is a member of the so-called 'iron-hearted myrtles' on account of the heavy, dark red heartwood. The limbs arch gracefully downward and can touch the ground. The species is also long-lived, and it is not uncommon to see 100-year-old trees growing in urban gardens. In the wild on coastal cliffs they can live for about one thousand years. The undersides of the leathery, oblong leaves are densely clothed with white hairs. The blossoms, locally called *kahika*, seem to smother the branches with a brilliant display of crimson, though numerous cultivars offer variations in flower colour including orange, white, pink and yellow, with peak flowering in mid- to late December.

The species has achieved an unusual, almost legendary renown in Wellington ever since the city council instructed the prestigious Wellington Club to mould the design of its new headquarters around the pohutukawa tree. Sparks have also flown in recent years over the policy to target pohutukawas in nature reserves, where they are classed as potentially invasive non-local natives, as commemorative trees planted by residents have been destroyed in the process. In their native range, the trees are under threat from the Australian brushtail possum, which feeds voraciously on the leaves.

METROSIDEROS
EXCELSA

Morus nigra
Black mulberry
Verona

These trees are a frequent sight along roadsides and in gardens around the city of Verona in northern Italy, including some superb mature examples. Both the black and closely related white mulberry were planted extensively in the flat cultivated plains that lie between Verona and Mantua, as they were once used as a food source for silkworms. The black mulberry is one of about 150 species and hybrid varieties worldwide that have been claimed to be mulberries. However, of these, fewer than 20 are accepted by a majority of botanists to constitute distinct species. Thought to be native to Iran, it has been in cultivation for such a long time that its precise natural range is uncertain.

The black mulberry is a deciduous tree growing to a height of 12m/39ft, but its canopy can also be spread widely – as much as 15m/50ft. The tree is reputed to enjoy considerable longevity, and older trees can take on a wonderfully gnarled and crooked appearance. However, claims of antiquity may be illusory because one method of propagation is by taking a length of old trunk and planting it in the ground using a technique called truncheoning. Mulberries bear broadly ovate, pointed leaves that are rough above and downy on the underside. The fruit, which ripens in autumn, somewhat resembles a blackberry, dark purple in colour, and made up of small, fleshy drupelets. It is edible and has a strong flavour.

Shakespeare is said to bear some responsibility for linking mulberry trees with Verona. He allegedly planted a tree in his garden in Stratford, and subsequently incorporated mulberries into several of his plays.

MORUS NIGRA

Olea europaea
European olive
Athens

Predictably, one does not have to travel far in Athens before catching sight of an olive tree. It can be said to be a symbol of the country, and on the Acropolis there stands a special olive tree that represents centuries of dedication and reverence to Athena, the patron goddess of the city. According to legend, the present-day tree is a descendant of one planted in a sacred grove in about 525 BC. The Acropolis was first built of olive wood, and when the Persian armies burnt it to the ground in 480 BC, the charred stump of the olive tree survived. Its seeds were subsequently planted across Attica. The oldest known surviving olive tree is as much as 5,000 years old (according to legend), standing in the village of Kolymvari in northern Crete, and is a national monument. Apparently it still produces olives. The trees can indeed reach a great age and there are more realistic, though unproven claims that some trees still producing fruit were planted more than 1,500 years ago.

By no stretch of the imagination does the European olive rank among the most beautiful of trees, but when old and gnarled it undoubtedly possesses a venerable aura that seems resistant to time and tide. These evergreen trees do not grow especially tall (rarely surpassing 10m/30ft), and they tend to retain a rather squat, rounded appearance. The trunk is often distorted, clothed with roughened, dark grey bark, and the boughs bear narrowly elliptical, leathery leaves with pointed tips. These are glossy and dark greyish-green above, rather paler below. The fragrant flowers are produced in late spring and are thoroughly insignificant, tiny, white and feathery. It is the familiar and much-valued fruit that commands attention in the autumn months. Known botanically as a drupe, with a fleshy outer part enclosing a hard stone or 'pit', the olive is initially green and turns a progressively darker purple as it ripens.

In Homeric Greece, the olive branch became a symbol of victory, with those defeated holding an olive branch to indicate that they were suing for peace. It was worn traditionally by both virgins and brides, and winning athletes were also crowned with a wreath made from leafy olive stems. The expression 'resting on ones laurels' followed, when the victor chose to bathe idly in the glory.

OLEA EUROPAEA

Peltophorum pterocarpum
Copper-pod
Mumbai

The city of Mumbai is graced with an abundance of trees, and this species is among the prettiest when in flower. Also known as yellow poinciana, it is grown as an ornamental along the roadsides, and can be found more or less everywhere throughout the city. It is traditionally planted in alternate arrangement with *Delonix regia* (see page 58) so as to provide a striking yellow-and-red effect when both are in bloom. If you want to see this floral spectacle at its best, take a trip along Hughes Road, one of the main arterial links in South Mumbai. There are also some splendid examples dotting the campus of the Indian Institute of Technology. Copper-pod flowers are comparatively simple but are produced in quantity, turning the trees into a mass of gold and forming pools of yellow on the ground beneath. It is known by a distinct common name, radhachura, in other Indian cities, notably Kolkata.

The tree is native to tropical southeast Asia but is grown as an ornamental in tropical regions around the world, and seems to have a reasonable tolerance of urban pollution. A semi-evergreen member of the bean family, it generally reaches a height of about 25m/82ft, sometimes extending to 50m/164ft in the wild, with a widely spreading, rounded canopy that provides useful shade. It produces large, compound leaves, up to 60cm/24in long, each divided into many pairs of dark green, oblong leaflets. The trees generally flower after about four years of growth, erupting into bloom in Mumbai between February and March, when the entire canopy becomes smothered with delicately perfumed blossoms that smell not unlike ripe grapes. The flowers are a glorious clear yellow, with crinkly petals and long orange-tipped stamens. Opening from rust-coloured buds, they are held in upright clusters up to 20cm/8in long, sometimes longer. Later come flat pods, which first turn red (hence the name 'copper-pod'), then blacken as they ripen. Each pod contains one to five seeds.

The wood is used in furniture-making, and the foliage provides a good fodder crop. The bark is valued in herbal medicine, both as an astringent and an analgesic. In Java the heartwood is rendered commercially to extract a brown dye used for colouring traditional batik work.

PELTOPHORUM
PTEROCARPUM

Phoenix dactylifera
Date palm
Riyadh

It is unlikely that the visitor to Saudi Arabia's capital city will take too long to spot what are commonly called date palms. They pretty much constitute an iconic feature of the place, and the best spots to admire them within the urban setting are Riyadh's public parks. Some of the finest specimen trees are scattered around King Abdullah Park, in the Malaz area, which stays open late at night and is well illuminated, so that you can enjoy the spectacle while escaping the worst of the daytime heat. A few blocks further north, Rawdah Park includes some mature *Phoenix dactylifera* bordering its open, grassy areas. There are also good selections in Olaya Park, Al Hamra Park towards the north of the city and bordering the lake of Salaam Park, which lies adjacent to the arterial King Fahd highway.

Phoenix dactylifera has been cultivated throughout history on account of its sweet, edible fruit throughout history, and is recorded in Arabia at least as far back in time as the 6th millennium BC. Although the original wild source of the tree is unknown, it almost certainly lay somewhere in the Middle East. These days, the species is found in most tropical and subtropical regions of the world. Date palms generally attain a height of 20–25m/66–82ft at maturity, and either grow singly or form a cluster of several trunks arising from a single root system. The familiar 'skyline' crown expands to a maximum of 10m/33ft, bearing huge evergreen leaves up to 6m/20ft in length. With separate male and female trees, the latter take up to eight years to bear fruit. In the wild, date palms are equipped for wind pollination, but in cultivation, where there may be only a single male tree grown, the females are more commonly pollinated manually. The resultant fruit, containing a single seed, is an elongated 'finger' as the Greek species name *dactylifera* suggests.

The seeds of the date palm possess a notorious longevity. Exactly for how long they can survive in storage is not known, but at least one seed discovered at Masada in Israel has been successfully germinated after inadvertently being stored for about 2,000 years.

PHOENIX
DACTYLIFERA

Phytolacca dioica
Ombú
Buenos Aires

Visit any green space in Buenos Aires and you are sure to encounter an ombú tree. A quite awesome example can be found in the Plaza Barrancas de Belgrano, a park close to the sea. A scarcely less impressive specimen dominates a plaza located about 6km/3.7mi to the southeast, bordering the Recoleta Cemetery. Another, which has become so distorted that it verges on the bizarre, stands in the Buenos Aires Botanical Garden, in the Palermo district. A little further out, south of the city centre, in Greater Buenos Aires, an eye-catching ombú can be found overshadowing the railway station of Banfield – strange-sounding because it is named after an English engineer.

Resembling a rubber tree, so occasionally the object of confusion, *Phytolacca dioica* is strictly indigenous to South America and is the only tree that occurs naturally on the pampas. Although essentially confined to the lowland plains, it can survive at altitudes from sea level up to 2,000m/6,560ft. Very fast-growing, it reaches a height of almost 20m/65ft and develops a massive canopy that can extend over 15m/49ft. The glossy, dark green, ovate leaves have prominent white or pink-tinged midribs. The trunk is often grotesquely swollen at the base, so the tree appears to be standing on a mound. The flowers are showy, arranged in pendulous clusters of greenish-white. Each contains both male and female parts, and matures into a poisonous fruit in the form of a small, black berry.

Technically, the ombú is an extremely large, multi-stemmed evergreen shrub related to pokeweed. In spite of its massive size, the trunk is not true wood, but very soft woody material that can be cut with a knife. It contains large amounts of water-storage tissue, making it remarkably fire-resistant. The species is thus well adapted to life on the pampas, which can suffer from chronic shortage of rainfall and, as a consequence, experiences frequent bush fires. It also produces a poisonous milky sap, effective at deterring animals that might otherwise browse on or bore into it. A welcome shade tree providing respite from the elements in otherwise featureless grasslands, the ombú is redolent of Argentina's gaucho culture.

PHYTOLACCA
DIOICA

Pinus halepensis
Aleppo pine
Jerusalem

One of four types of pine tree that grow in Israel, and known locally as Jerusalem pine, this species is actually indigenous to a large part of the Mediterranean region, extending from the Middle East westwards into southern France and Spain. It is among the four most common tree species planted in the various neighbourhoods around Jerusalem, in company with Mediterranean cypress, olive and red river gum. Some of the best specimen trees can be seen in the Jerusalem Botanical Gardens. A few miles west of the city centre, in the Jerusalem mountains, there are also some fine, mature examples in the Hamasrek Reserve. In times past, Aleppo pine used to grow extensively in natural woodlands in Israel, but now it can only be found in very isolated spots.

This is not the prettiest or most eye-catching of trees; nevertheless, Aleppo pine is very much a part of the city's landscape. It is a rather scraggy evergreen conifer capable of growing where few other trees would readily survive. Strongly drought-tolerant, it thrives on rocky slopes with thin soil, especially in desert surroundings. It can live for up to eighty years, sometimes more, usually reaching a height of about 8m/26ft, growing in a more or less even pyramid shape, at least when young, before becoming increasingly irregular in outline as it matures. The trees tend to lean, although the trunk is generally straight, covered with greyish, flaking, resinous bark, and also shows a tendency to divide. The foliage is quite sparse, in the form of mid-green needles up to 10cm/4in long, generally in clusters of two. The immature fruits take the form of green cones, 6–7cm/2½–2¾in long, which ripen over a period of two years, progressively turning reddish-brown.

In ancient times, *Pinus halepensis* was the sacred tree of the Egyptian sun god Aten, and the copious resiny sap that can be extracted from the tree was once employed for embalming Egyptian pharaohs. It is also alleged to be the 'oil tree' mentioned in the Old Testament's Book of Isaiah. In a more modern context, the resin transforms Greek wine into retsina.

PINUS HALEPENSIS

Pinus nigra
Black pine
Nice

Just as *Pinus pinea* is a living symbol of Rome, *Pinus nigra* may well qualify as a species symbolic of many cities across southern Europe, from Spain to Turkey. Also known as the Austrian pine and the Corsican pine, it is a common sight in Nice, mingled with *Quercus ilex* (holm oak). One particularly striking veteran awaits discovery in the Colline du Château Park. Other mature examples stand in the Mont Boron Park, the Mont Vinaigrier Park on the eastern outskirts of the city and in the Estienne d'Orves Parc Naturel. Each of these sites offers a rich combination of olive, oak and pine, and if one is prepared to drive for an hour or so north of Nice, there is a forest of black pines in the Mercantour National Park.

Its native range lies chiefly in Turkey, where it occurs at altitudes of up to 2,000m/6,600ft, but it is also found on the slopes of the Apennines in southern Italy. Not to be confused with Japanese black pine (*Pinus thunbergii*), this impressive evergreen conifer reaches maturity after about 80 years, and can live for 500 years or more. It is hardy and frost-tolerant, and provided that it benefits from full sun, the species grows fairly rapidly to a height of between 30–50m/100–164ft, with a spread of up to 15m/50ft. Maintaining a tall, pyramid shape during development, at maturity it becomes characteristically flat-topped. The trunk is straight, clothed in grey-brown bark that flakes away in plates, becoming increasingly cracked into long vertical fissures with age. The needles are bundled in pairs, and can be pale or dark green. New male and female cones emerge on the same tree in May and June. Female cones ripen about eighteen months after pollination (by wind), shedding dark grey seeds with yellowish winged extensions in the winter months.

Some of the most magnificent examples standing today, reaching just short of 45m/148ft in height, are found in the mountainous Laruns commune, in the Pyrénées-Atlantiques department of southwest France.

PINUS NIGRA

Pinus pinea
Italian stone pine
Rome

Among the many kinds of pine that occur around the world, this species is quintessentially Italian, and is undoubtedly the one most closely associated with Rome. Also known as the umbrella pine on account of its profile, the tree has become an enduring symbol of the city. It lines historic streets such as the famous Via dei Fori Imperiali, which connects the Piazza Venezia with the Colosseum, and it populates parts of the old Appian Way that once carried travellers south as far as Brindisi. It is worth visiting the Palatine and Aventine Hills, where some fine specimen trees provide welcome shade as you gaze out over the spectacle of the city. There are some grandiose veteran stone pines to be discovered at the Terme di Caracalla and in the Parco Borghese.

The species is actually native to the coastal areas of the Mediterranean region, but was introduced to north Africa at some time in distant history, and is now to all intents and purposes naturalised there too. The tree has been maintained in cultivation since prehistoric times for at least 6,000 years, chiefly for its edible nuts, but it is now more commonly planted as an ornamental in parks and gardens and bordering urban streets. Away from the urban environment there still exist a number of stone pine forests scattered around southern Europe.

Stone pine is an evergreen conifer that grows about 1m/3ft a year, exceptionally reaching a height of more than 25m/82ft. When mature, it is architecturally beautiful, typically with a broad, flat-topped crown borne on a tall, thick trunk, clothed in reddish-brown, deeply fissured bark. At maturity, its leaves form paired, dark green needles, each as much as 20cm/8in long, although on young trees they are much shorter and a bluish-green. The small pollen-producing cones are yellow and cylindrical, while the larger, ovate seed cones turn from green to a shiny pale brown. These take three years to reach maturity, longer than those of any other pine species, and the seeds when ripe are unusually large. They are the favoured basis of pesto, but these days are increasingly under attack from the western conifer seed bug, a sap-sucking pest introduced inadvertently to Italy in the 1990s.

PINUS PINEA

Platanus x *acerifolia*
London plane
London

One hardly needs to point out special places in London to spot the London plane: it accounts for more than half of all the city's trees. Though one of the more familiar sights in England's capital, the London plane is not actually a native European tree, but rather is believed to have been a hybrid of two species originating on separate continents, *Platanus orientalis* (oriental plane) and *Platanus occidentalis* (American sycamore). The London origins can be traced back to the mid-17th century when a specimen was planted in a famous nursery garden in Vauxhall, south London.

The Latin name of this tree refers to the shape of the leaves, which are reminiscent of those of the sycamore (*Acer pseudoplatanus*). More distinctive, however, is the curiously patterned bark, which develops into a flaky camouflage of greys, olives and creams. Supported by a robust trunk, London plane can reach a height of 35m/115ft, and its spreading branches make it appear almost as broad as it is tall, although on London streets the trees tend to be inelegantly pruned back. They bear tiny greenish male flowers, and red females that appear separately on the same tree, usually in May, producing copious amounts of pollen, causing frequent health problems for Londoners prone to allergies. The fruit takes the form of little greenish, burr-like balls that turn brown and disintegrate at maturity, releasing tiny feathery seeds into the wind for dispersal.

The popularity of London planes for urban planting burgeoned during the Industrial Revolution, when many cities, including London, were permanently begrimed with soot from coal-burning, and smog had become a fact of life (though 'smog' was yet to be coined as a portmanteau of smoke and fog). The plane-tree-lined boulevards of Paris were viewed with increasing envy by Londoners clamouring for similar greenery that proved able to withstand air pollution and adapt to the conditions created by urban expansion.

PLATANUS X ACERIFOLIA

Podocarpus latifolius
Broad-leaf yellowwood
Johannesburg

This tree is not among the biggest of the *Podocarpus* species, perhaps one of the reasons it is well represented along pavements and sidewalks in Johannesburg. Some of the most memorable examples are those lining Katherine Street, which extends from Marlboro Drive. As South Africa's national tree it also features prominently in many of the city parks. One particularly fine specimen can be discovered in Zoo Lake Park, situated in Saxonwold. There is also a grove of the trees, planted in the 1970s, close to the main entrance of the Johannesburg Botanical Garden. Among Joburg residents, smaller-growing cultivars such as 'Ubuntu' have become popular as Christmas trees and as garden ornamentals. In company with other species of *Podocarpus*, the broad-leaf yellowwood is now on the list of nationally protected trees.

Indigenous to eastern and southern regions of South Africa, from sea level up to 2,000m/6,600ft, but also occurring to a limited extent as far north as Zimbabwe, *Podocarpus latifolius* is best suited to life in forests and open coastal bush lands where there is good rainfall and some protection from fires. It is a majestic evergreen that is slow-growing but can reach a height of 30m/100ft. It displays a pyramid-shaped profile borne up on a trunk clothed with greyish bark that becomes fissured as it matures, and peels away in strips. The branches are densely arranged and typically begin close to the ground. They bear glossy, strap-like leaves up to 10cm/4in long, which compared with those of other *Podocarpus* species are quite broad, hence the name *latifolius*. Pale green at first, they become progressively darker. The species has separate male and female trees. Male cones, which appear in late summer, resemble little catkins, while female cones develop rounded greyish-blue seeds attached to fleshy, berry-like receptacles that turn purple as they mature in late winter. The highly valued yellow timber is hard and durable, but the extent of commercial logging has placed the species at serious risk of extinction.

PODOCARPUS
LATIFOLIUS

Populus nigra 'Italica'
Lombardy poplar
Amsterdam

In a country which is rather flat by nature of its geography, any tree that is tall and statuesque will tend to stand out impressively from a distance. Two types of poplar tend to grow in urban areas of Amsterdam: the hybrid Canadian poplar and the famous Lombardy poplar. Close to 14,500 poplar trees can be found within the confines of Amsterdam, so you needn't look far to discover one. *Populus nigra* 'Italica' is especially striking because of its slender, usually plume-like profile. On Apollolaan stand two monumental specimens that have been growing for around a century and have reached an exceptional height of almost 35m/115ft, with a girth approaching 6m/20ft. Scarcely smaller, another pair of giants bracket an archway in Jan Luijken Street. The mightiest of the hybrid Canadian poplars in Amsterdam is to be found in the famous Vondel Park, southwest of the centre, coming in at nearly 39m/128ft tall. The park also holds a comparatively diminutive Lombardy poplar, at a mere 15m/50ft in height.

Native to Europe, southwest and central Asia and parts of North Africa, the true Lombardy poplar 'Italica' is thought to have been hybridised in Lombardy, northern Italy, in the 17th century. It is fast-growing with a fairly short lifespan of 40–50 years, after which it becomes unstable and ranks of the trees can potentially fall in a domino effect. The species is also susceptible to a range of diseases that may cause disfigurement. Amsterdam can count itself lucky to have such fine exceptions to the rule.

It is characterised by branches that start close to the ground and lie almost parallel with the main trunk. The bark is dark brown, but may appear black from a distance, hence the name. In all other respects it resembles typical *Populus nigra*, dark brown bark, knobbly twigs and triangular leaves with extended tips. Female trees have yellow catkins and produce fluffy seeds reminiscent of cotton. True 'Italica' always bears male catkins; these are red and appear before the leaf buds open.

POPULUS NIGRA
'ITALICA'

Prunus x *yedoensis*
Yoshino cherry
Kyoto

Finding cherry trees in Kyoto is not a problem, but timing your visit is rather more critical. The trees are in blossom from late March until early April, and undoubtedly the best way to see them in all their finery is to visit the temples and shrines. One of the first places on your itinerary should be Kyoto Gyoen, a park surrounding the Imperial Palace. It is also worth seeking out a disused railway line between sections of the Lake Biwa Canal, running from the harbour to Onjoji-cho Park. The tracks are still there, but you can walk the length of them and on either side is an avenue of cherry trees. Both banks of the canal are considered to be excellent viewing places where you can also pause for a while at one of the many small cafés that line the waterway. About two hundred flowering cherries stand in the grounds of Nanzen-ji Temple, which can be accessed from Keage Station, but more or less any of the city's temples offer a similar vista. Flag down a taxi and go a short distance into the hills overlooking Kyoto, where there is another breathtaking array in the grounds of Konkaikomyo-ji Temple. For cherry tree magic of a different kind, try Maruyama Park after dark. The park includes a quite famous weeping cherry that is illuminated as night falls.

The Yoshino cherry, as such, is not a species indigenous to Japan, but is actually a hybrid of two different species that was given its formal name in 1901. It grows as a fairly small deciduous tree, reaching a height of 6–12m/20–39ft, with a broad canopy and reddish-brown bark. The leaves can extend up to 15cm/6in long and 7cm/3in broad, with a serrated margin. Often reddish as they emerge, they turn dark green as they mature. The five-petalled white or pallid pink flowers, for which the tree is rightly renowned, emerge singly, though in profusion, along the branches, usually before the leaves appear, giving out a faint fragrance of almond. The little black cherries are not particularly sweet or palatable, except to birds.

Prunus x *yedoensis* has gained worldwide popularity as an ornamental tree since it was first introduced from Japan in the early 1900s. Although formally named in 1901 (Yedo being an old name for Tokyo), the origin of this hybrid has long been a mystery.

PRUNUS X YEDOENSIS

Pterocarya fraxinifolia
Caucasian wingnut
Amsterdam

As its name implies, this tree is native to the Caucasus region of eastern Europe, extending into parts of western Asia. Since it was first brought into urban cultivation in France in 1874, it has been introduced to countries across western Europe. The Caucasian wingnut belongs to the same family as *Juglans regia* (common walnut), and is probably at its most attractive in July, when the extraordinarily long catkins have fully extended. Amsterdam's grandest specimen, thought to be over one hundred years old and claiming a massive girth of nearly 5m/16ft, stands in the garden of the Rijks Museum. It has been estimated that its trunk expands by nearly 50cm/20in a year. Another specimen tree of similar stature is located in Wertheim Park, its branches spreading far over the adjacent canal. A smaller, but no less striking example, somehow managing to grow sideways at an almost impossible angle, can be found in Sarphati Park. Planted in 1885, its roots have weakened, and at some moment in its long life it has partly toppled over, yet it continues growing.

In its native environment, *Pterocarya fraxinifolia* is generally found growing in warm climates, on riverbanks, in almost boggy soil, and thus in cultivation it is best suited to places with mild winters and damp summers. It is an impressive, broadly spreading deciduous tree with an almost triangular profile, a fairly massive trunk base and roughly fissured bark. The leaves are no less striking, since each can extend to more than 60cm/24in in length. Made up of pinnate, pointed leaflets without stalks, each individual leaflet is itself up to 15cm/6in long.

The Caucasian wingnut gains its unusual name from the shape of its fruits, which have semicircular wings and mature in late summer to early autumn. It is among the more ancient and primitive members of the walnut family, indicated by the fact that its seeds are dispersed by wind action. The more highly evolved walnuts and related hickory species, by contrast, generate edible nuts that are dispersed by animals.

PTEROCARYA
FRAXINIFOLIA

Quercus ilex
Holm oak
Nice

With its striking appearance as a mature tree, *Quercus ilex* is indigenous to the wider Mediterranean region and graces many southern European towns and cities, alongside familiar palms and stone pines. Since Roman times the tree has been an indispensable source of hard, durable timber, though these days it is no less valued as an ornamental, providing welcome shade. Not surprisingly it makes a majestic evergreen spectacle in many of the parks and gardens of Nice. Close to the city centre, in Place Garibaldi, some fine examples conveniently shade the tramway stop and provide a backdrop to the statue of the great Italian General. The municipal botanic gardens, located at 78 Corniche Fleurie, contain an extensive range of Mediterranean tree species, including *Quercus ilex*. Travel a short way out of town to the Grande Corniche Nature Park, and you can see many more mature examples in a forest setting.

Holm oak, also known as holly or evergreen oak, can reach a substantial 25m/82ft in height, carried up on a stout trunk bearing wide, spreading branches. When fully formed it has a regular, rounded profile with slightly downward-pointing branches that sweep low to the ground. The tree can live for 200 years and, in common with other oak species, the limbs often become gnarled at maturity. It earns its botanical name from the shape of the young leaves that, on lower branches, bear spiny teeth reminiscent of those on true holly (*Ilex aquifolium*). The leaves are generally renewed annually, and display a silvery-grey colour when unfolding. In springtime the trees can also look golden due to large numbers of yellowish male catkins. Holm oak is wind-pollinated, and the resultant fruit is an acorn in a knobbly grey cup, slightly smaller than those of deciduous oaks. The acorns fall to the ground in autumn and are dispersed by animals.

Although Mediterranean in origin, it can grow further north in many more temperate parts of Europe, where it copes reasonably well with low temperatures, although it does not tolerate severe frost. Allegedly Roman emperors wore crowns that were often fashioned from holm oak leaves, rather than laurel.

QUERCUS ILEX

Quercus robur
Pedunculate oak
Berlin

Also known as the English oak, this species is a common sight and grows wild throughout much of Europe. It is also extensively cultivated, and in the city of Berlin there are so many particularly fine monumental examples of pedunculate oak, one is almost spoilt for choice. One such specimen tree stands near the main Köpenicker Chaussee thoroughfare in the Rummelsburg area, beside the Spree River. Another example well worth seeking out stands in a street named An der Wuhlheide, in the Köpenick district; and an extraordinary-looking specimen can be found in Bellevue Park in the same area. A short way to the east, in the Tegel locality, there are yet more fine, mature examples to be discovered. One, the so-called 'Dicke Marie' stands in Nordspitze Tegeler See. Another massive tree, also venerable enough to have earnt a name, the *Humboldteiche*, with a partly hollowed trunk, stands in the Schloss Park.

These trees breathe ruggedness and strength; the oldest can live for more than 1,000 years. They can easily reach a height of 35m/115ft. The trunk, with a girth of 12m/39ft or so, supports often jaggedly distorted limbs and a broad, open crown. The deeply furrowed bark of the lower branches may become populated with epiphytic ferns that take root in its crevices. In common with most oak species, *Quercus robur* is deciduous; oak leaves are often the last to fall in mixed woodland, clinging to the branches until well into December. The leaves are lobed and short-stalked. Yellow male catkins appear as the tree comes into leaf between early May and June; separate female flowers develop into the familiar acorn resting in its knobbly cup. The term pedunculate refers to the distinctively long stalks that bear the acorns.

The pedunculate oak is of considerable ecological importance, playing host to numerous insects, and its acorns constitute a significant food source for various small mammals and birds. The trees are often propagated in the wild by squirrels and jays that bury the acorns for future use and then forget them. A high economic value is placed on the hard, durable timber. In Germany, the oak symbolises the nation's strength and stability, and an oak branch is displayed on the reverse of some German-issue euro coins.

QUERCUS
ROBUR

Quercus virginiana
Southern live oak
Tallahassee

If there is a single species of tree indelibly linked with the culture and romance of the Deep South, it must surely be the live oak. Indigenous to the southeastern United States and parts of northern Mexico, these iconic trees create a lasting impression for visitors to the city of Tallahassee, where they abound. One of the most massive and quite glorious examples is to be discovered in Elinor Klapp-Phipps Park, which lies a little way to the north of Highway 10, extending out from the city centre. Standing by a trail deep in the Florida wetlands, this massive oak drips with Spanish moss and positively exudes the spirit of Confederate Dixie and Scarlett O'Hara. Another setting in which to find some splendid examples, again reached at the northern end of the city, is the Alfred B. Maclay Gardens State Park. Pre-civil war, this area constituted the western end of a cotton plantation called Live Oak Plantation.

Quercus virginiana is a large, graceful tree, and it can survive for up to 250 years, although it is claimed that some trees are much older. Occasionally live oaks reach as much as 30m/100ft in height, but generally grow to only about half that size. The species has one of the broadest, most sprawling canopies of any oak, extending in some cases to 45m/148ft in width. The branches, which sweep downward before turning up at their tips, sometimes require additional support because of their remarkable span. The trunk is sturdy, with deeply furrowed, dark brownish-grey bark. The leaves are coarse and leathery, not unlike those typical of European oaks but with a more regular outline. Although the tree is considered evergreen, the leaves fall in spring just as the new foliage unfurls. Greenish male and female catkins appear and pollination is by wind during April. The resultant fruits are shiny brown, pointed acorns, which often become blackened at the tip, and rest in a knobbly greyish-green cup.

The long silvery tendrils of Spanish moss that hang from the branches of many live oaks actually belong to an epiphytic flowering plant, *Tillandsia usneoides*. Like other 'air plants', it can absorb water and nutrients from the atmosphere.

QUERCUS
VIRGINIANA

Sabal palmetto
Cabbage palm
Columbia

Also known locally as the blue palmetto or Carolina palmetto, this is one of fifteen species of palmetto palm. The native range of the tree, more or less restricted to the coastal plains of the southern United States, extends from South Carolina to Texas via Florida. It also includes Cuba and the Bahamas. Cabbage palm is well suited to use in street planting, but the trees found within the city confines are not generally grown from seed because they take a long time to become established. Instead they are more often dug up and transplanted from the wild.

Borne on a tall, slender but remarkably strong trunk that can reach a height of 15m/49ft or more, the tree bears a spread of large fan-like leaves at its crown, each extending up to 1m/3ft across. The leaves are described botanically as being costapalmate, meaning that each possesses a distinct midrib, from which radiate numerous leaflets. The presence of the midrib distinguishes the leaves of the *Sabal palmetto* from other fan palms.

Palmetto palms are members of an ancient group of fairly primitive trees that date back some 80 million years to the Cretaceous period. In the southern American states cabbage palm presents a familiar sight, and has been adopted as the official tree of both South Carolina and Florida. The tree is easy to maintain and tolerant not only of frost and periodic snow, but also of drought and salt pollution, though not of flooding by sea water. Attributable to the fact that the trunks are constructed not of wood but of fibrous material, the trees are also remarkably flexible, and thus can withstand periodic hurricanes.

In the wild, the trunks of cabbage palms appear spiky because after the leaves die they do not fall away cleanly, and instead the leaf bases persist as what are locally known as 'bootjacks', resembling devices used in bygone days to remove boots. However, when planted in urban settings the leaf bases are generally shaved off, leaving a smooth appearance.

The tree is commonly called the cabbage palm because it produces an immature palm 'heart' in the new fronds which is said to taste rather like cabbage. The removal of the hearts is strongly discouraged, however, because doing so damages the tree.

SABAL PALMETTO

Salix babylonica
Weeping willow
Eindhoven

The true origin of the species is not entirely clear, but it is considered to be native to areas of northern China. Over time, ever since it was 'exported' westwards along the ancient silk roads thousands of years ago, it has proved universally popular for planting as a graceful ornamental providing good shade. One such place is Eindhoven. In the main Stadswandel Park, which lies a short walk south from the city centre, you will find two particularly fine examples. Their height has not been determined recently, but they are over 12m/39ft tall, and each has attained a girth that comfortably exceeds 2m/7ft. Weeping willows can in fact be found in almost all the city's parks, including Severijn Park in the Gestel district. They are also dotted along the banks of the main Eindhovensch Canal.

Salix babylonica is undoubtedly best suited to moist conditions, next to water. The pendulous 'weeping' form of the tree is actually a cultivated variety, which is instantly recognisable by its long slender branches that sweep down gracefully and often meet the ground. The trees display rapid growth, and can reach a height of 25m/82ft, but their life expectancy is comparatively short, rarely more than 60 years. The greyish-brown bark is rough and furrowed and the leaves are narrowly lance-shaped with long, pointed tips. Trees are either male or female, bearing inconspicuous catkins each about 2cm/¾in long, with a rather fuzzy appearance, and pollination is generally performed by bees. The fruit takes the form of a cluster of little capsules, which open by valves to reveal fluffy, cottony seeds that ripen in May and June.

To dispense with a myth, it is unlikely that these trees ever grew by the waters of Babylon, or that the exiled Israelites necessarily wept beside them! The trees named as willows in the Old Testament of the Bible were almost certainly a species of poplar that droops and has willow-like leaves. In reality the scientific name *Salix babylonica* arose as a simple misunderstanding on the part of the botanist, Carl Linnaeus, who originally coined the title.

SALIX BABYLONICA

Salix matsudana
Peking willow
Beijing

Salix matsudana vies for popularity as an urban favourite with *Salix babylonica* (weeping willow). Native to the same part of northern China, the two species are regarded as synonymous by some. Both are widely used in Beijing as street trees, for shade and also as a way to combat the capital's notorious smog. However, in springtime Beijing experiences a 'snowstorm' of cottony seeds drifting down from the tens of thousands of female willows. The fluff causes respiratory problems and, when piled high, even represents a fire hazard. In 1994 the authorities responded by launching a project to replace many of the female trees with imported male trees. Unfortunately for allergy sufferers, only 10% of the gender balance has so far been adjusted. Peking willows can be found in a particularly iconic setting, complete with a traditional red bridge, in the Changpu River Park. Many other attractive examples can be viewed in the Olympic Forest Park, at the northern end of the Beijing central axis. Created in 2008, the park contains more than half a million native trees.

A fairly small deciduous tree, *Salix matsudana* grows rapidly and can reach 8–10m/26–33ft in height, with a 5m/16ft spread of branches that characteristically grow close to the trunk before fanning out horizontally. Favouring moist soil, it develops an airy, open crown, and bears narrow, light green lance-shaped leaves, up to 15cm/6in long, with serrated margins. Inconspicuous male and female catkins are produced on separate trees.

Various cultivars of *Salix matsudana* are also popular as urban ornamentals, particularly the dragon's claw or corkscrew willow, but tend to have a limited lifespan and generally only flourish for ten to fifteen years. In Beijing, trees of any type tend to be planted much closer together than would be considered appropriate in other cities of the world, a practice that may trace back to regulations enacted by Kublai Khan in the 13th century, when roadside trees served as winter snow markers.

SALIX MATSUDANA

Sequoiadendron giganteum
Giant redwood
Reno

This truly awesome species of evergreen tree is not indigenous to the desert city of Reno or even Nevada. Its native range, at altitudes above 1,400m, is in neighbouring California on west-facing slopes in the mountains and valleys of the Sierra Nevada. The species appears to thrive in the state of Nevada, however, not least because of the cold winter months there, to which it is well suited. Since Reno first expanded as a metropolis, giant redwood trees have been planted around its neighbourhoods and in urban parks, although as they are shallow-rooting they are not approved as street trees. Giant redwood can be discovered at the Reno Arboretum, in Idlewild Park, where it is a feature at several points around the tree walk. Alas, none of those to be discovered in Reno amounts to anything other than youthful. Not until they pass 100 years do they technically reach a vintage approaching maturity.

Distinct from coastal redwood, the trees are capable of attaining at least 90m/300ft in height and are known from ring counts to have a potential lifespan of 3,500 years, which makes this species one of the oldest living things on earth. The trunk is a straight column clothed with bark that is thick, fibrous and furrowed. Because a tree of such a size cannot draw water beyond a certain height from ground level, giant redwoods have developed small aerial roots that absorb moisture from the atmosphere. The leaves are insignificant in size, and are arranged in spirals on the shoots. The trees start to generate cones after about twelve years, produced mainly in the upper parts of the canopy. A large, mature tree may bear more than 10,000 cones at any one time, capable of shedding up to 400,000 winged seeds in a year.

This is the only living species of its genus, and with a currently decreasing population it is considered endangered. To witness the real giants among *Sequoiadendron* trees you have to head down the freeway from Reno into California. A record-breaker named the Hyperion, the world's largest known living tree, towers above a guarded location in Redwood National Park, and stands at just short of 116m/380ft, the length of a soccer pitch.

Sorbus aucuparia
Rowan
Stockholm

Following close behind the ubiquitous limes and maples, rowans rank a prominent third among the city's most frequently planted street tree. One of the best places to see the trees is on Djurgården, an island in central Stockholm. Be prepared for some serious walking if you want to explore the park further, as it stretches over 10km/6mi to Ulriksdal in the north. The common name rowan in fact derives from its Swedish equivalent *rönn*, a word with Old Norse roots meaning 'to redden'. The species does not present a grand, monumental spectacle, but it serves as a fairly robust and attractive choice for city streets, parks and gardens, and throughout Europe it has become one of the more significant members of the so-called 'urban forest'. What it lacks in spring colour it more than makes up for with its mass of bright red berries and brilliant autumn foliage.

Sorbus aucuparia is a slender deciduous tree that reaches a maximum height of 20m/66ft, often much less, and it can live for as many as 200 years. Although it is commonly called 'mountain ash', it is neither related to ash trees (*Sorbus* belongs to the rose family), nor is its scope limited to mountains. The range is extensive across various habitats throughout Europe and southwest Asia. The trunk bears smooth, silvery-grey bark, and the pinnate leaves are composed of up to 35 oval leaflets with serrated edges. The five-petalled flowers appear in late spring and they carry both male and female parts, forming dense, flattish, cream-coloured clusters. Pollination is by insects, and the resulting scarlet pomes contain seeds spread mainly by birds that feast on the fruit.

A curious feature of these trees lies in their synchronous masting – the fruits ripen and are shed usually in August, but at more or less the same time all over Scandinavia. There is a piece of old but popular folklore in Sweden that the *rönn* will not bear a heavy load of fruit and a heavy load of snow in the same season. The rowan has also been considered a magical tree, and has long been planted near houses to protect against evil.

SORBUS
AUCUPARIA

Syzygium smithii
Lilly-pilly
Melbourne

This evergreen rainforest tree has been in use in Melbourne since the early 1900s as it adapts well to a range of soil types, including the clay soils found in different parts of the city. It can be employed as a freestanding avenue tree but will also tolerate being pruned vigorously for hedging. It is also known to be fire-retardant. The species should be fairly easy to find by a visitor as it is one of the top ten most popular trees for planting. Rows of them, frequently mixed with *Acer*, line Millswyn Street and Moore Street, both near the Royal Botanic Gardens, and on the other side of the Yarra River, Flinders Lane and Royal Lane.

In its native range, *Syzygium smithii* (sometimes known by the older name *Acmena smithii*) is found in wooded areas bordering estuaries and creeks in eastern coastal regions from Victoria to Queensland, where it is best suited to growing in full sun or light shade. But it can also be found at higher altitudes in the Blue Mountains, where it is partly frost-resistant. It develops as a smallish tree, usually about 15m/49ft in height, and can live for up to 200 years, although in exposed areas it may remain a shrub. With a dense crown and an upright, oval profile, it is often multi-stemmed and can branch from close to ground level. The finely roughened, flaky bark is a rich reddish-brown. Leaves are either lance-shaped or more broadly ovate, up to 11cm/4¼in long, and dark glossy green or sometimes variegated. The small, white flowers, produced in springtime, are formed from an elongated trumpet-shaped receptacle with a rim of protruding stamens. Following fertilisation by bees and other insects, large bunches of small white or pinkish-purple berries develop in early winter, suspended on long stalks and each containing a single seed.

The fruit of *Syzygium smithii* can remain on the tree for many weeks and is popular with a range of birds and mammals, including brushtail possums and flying foxes. It is also a well-known source of 'bush tucker', with little flavour and edible either raw or cooked.

SYZYGIUM SMITHII

Tilia cordata
Small-leaved lime
Berlin

This is the prettiest among the thirty or so species of lime tree that can be found across the northern hemisphere. It has long been intimately associated with Berlin, having lent its name to the Unter den Linden (literally 'under the linden trees'), the famous boulevard that stretches 1.5km/1mi from the site of the old Berliner Stadtschloss westwards to the Brandenburg Gate. The boulevard was first planted in 1647 by the Elector of Brandenburg, Friedrich Wilhelm, who had six rows of trees laid out to replace an old bridle path leading to the imperial hunting grounds in the Tiergarten. Friedrich Wilhelm protected the trees by stipulating that anyone deliberately damaging a tree would forfeit a hand. The order must have been reasonably effective because a woodcut dated 1691 reveals quite sturdy trees gracing what had already become known as Linden Allee. In 1820 the rows were reduced to four, and in the following century these were restricted exclusively to limes. Today, some of those original trees, which can live for 500 years or more, still line the grassy pedestrian mall beside the dual carriageway.

Broad and statuesque, *Tilia cordata* can reach a height of 35m/115ft. 'Small' is strictly a reference to the leaves, which are more diminutive than those of other species, and heart-shaped in profile, hence the name *cordata*. Compared with other limes, this one flowers quite late, in June and July, erupting with masses of deliciously scented, creamy blossom much loved by bees. The flowers are suspended in clusters from the tips of the branches. They are followed by bunches of little pea-shaped fruits with leafy wings, which fall to the ground in October.

It was Marlene Dietrich who once sang: 'As long as the old trees blossom on Unter den Linden, nothing can overcome us, Berlin remains Berlin'. Sadly, many are being lost to the ravages of pollution, and some of the trees had to be felled in 2012 to make way for a new metro line beneath Unter den Linden, but young trees were planted in their place.

TILIA CORDATA

Ulmus glabra
Wych elm
Stockholm

As if by a miracle, pockets of mature elm trees sometimes escape the effects of Dutch elm disease. One that has proved somewhat more resistant, and has the widest European range of any, is the wych elm, though Stockholm is at its most northerly natural limits. It gains its name not through any association with witches, but through the corruption of an old English word 'wicker', which means strong but flexible. The city hosts some truly monumental examples of this tree. One of the grandest with a girth of nearly 5.5m/18ft, it was measured to be a mighty 39m/128ft tall nearly ten years ago, which is just about as tall as they get.

Ulmus glabra has a broad, elegant profile. The branches characteristically rise from near the base and then angle upwards. The grey bark is at first smooth, hence the epithet *glabra* (meaning 'smooth' in Latin), only taking on a roughened and fissured appearance when it reaches maturity. Elm species can be tricky to separate one from another, but a close inspection of the wych elm leaf reveals an odd distinguishing feature. The base of the leaf, as in most elms, is asymmetric, but in this case the larger lobe wraps over the leaf stalk, partly hiding it. Tiny wind-pollinated flowers appear in springtime. Devoid of petals, each flower consists of naked, reddish stamens surrounding the female parts. The fruit is a broadly winged samara bearing a single seed.

In May 1971 an impassioned dispute known as the Battle of the Elms took place in Stockholm. The environmental group Alternativ Stad staged a protest against the felling of thirteen wych elms that stood in the way of a new metro station entrance about to be built in Kungsträdgården. There ensued a much-publicised stand-off until eventually the Stockholm authorities gave way and chose another site. The trees were spared, but it was a close call: chainsaw marks are still visible on some of the trunks.

ULMUS GLABRA

Xanthostemon chrysanthus
Golden penda
Cairns

Indigenous to coastal rainforests in northeastern Queensland, the native range of this species is restricted to an area between Lamb Range down to Cardwell, a stretch of about 200km/124mi. Golden penda is particularly pretty and has been adopted as the floral emblem of Cairns. Not surprisingly, it is one of the more popular choices among those officially listed in a residential tree programme, and has been planted extensively both in gardens and streets around the city. Because of its restricted height, it is suitable for use where there are overhead power lines. You will readily discover the trees along Cairns roadsides, but there are also fine examples on the campus of James Cook University and in the Cairns Botanic Gardens.

In the wild, golden penda generally achieves a height of about 15m/49ft, with a spread of 5–8m/16–26ft. It can, however, be quite rigorously pruned, and when cultivated in an urban setting it is typically kept small and bushy. Belonging to the myrtle family, it is evergreen and has rough brown bark with narrowly ovate leaves, glossy and dark green, arranged in whorls along the stems. The tree normally flowers within the first two or three years in tropical areas, and the blossoms can emerge several times a year, generally after periods of heavy rain. Arising at the ends of twigs, the blossoms are very conspicuous, looking from a distance like spiky golden puffballs. They do not have true petals – their allure is due instead to the many long, bright yellow stamens emerging from a calyx of small greenish sepals. They are also very attractive to birds. The fruit is a small green capsule that ripens to become brown and woody.

Golden penda has gained comparable popularity as an ornamental in other towns and cities in Queensland, including the capital Brisbane, where it was elected as the theme plant for World Expo 88. The scientific name *Xanthostemon* is descriptive and comes from two Greek words meaning 'yellow' and 'thread', together referring to the showy flowers.

XANTHOSTEMON
CHRYSANTHUS

Zelkova serrata
Keyaki
Miyakonojo

In common with several other Japanese towns and cities, Miyakonojo has chosen the zelkova as one of its symbols. It carries strong cultural and historical associations, and is said to embody the essential grace-and-strength qualities of the growing city. Perhaps predictably, the zelkova vies for popularity with the flowering cherry in Miyakonojo's humid, subtropical climate that suits the species well. There is a particularly fine example in Kanbashira Park and elsewhere, the Mochio-Sekinoo Prefectural Natural Park includes some beautiful mature zelkovas, although the park is principally renowned for its waterfalls and cherry trees.

Native to Japan, *Zelkova serrata* is a deciduous tree that in the wild can grow to about 30m/98ft in height, though in an urban setting rarely surpasses 20m/66ft, with a potential lifespan of more than 500 years, and it has become popular as an ornamental that develops brilliant autumnal colours of orange and red. Tolerant of moderate levels of pollution, it will grow in poor soils and requires little water, all of which are assets for urban planting. The main trunk tends to be short, soon dividing into a multiplicity of low branches that at first grow upright and then spread into a broad, rounded canopy. The mature bark tends to be greyish-white and flaky, revealing an orange layer beneath. The young brownish-purple twigs bear oblong to ovate leaves, roughened on the surface with serrated margins, hence the Latin name *serrata*. Inconspicuous greenish flowers appear in springtime, males and females on different sections of the branch. The fruit is a small oval drupe, maturing from green to brown.

Zelkova wood is used to make traditional furniture and for turning particularly fine carved ornaments. The species has been proposed as a replacement for the American elm in the US, as it shows resistance to Dutch elm disease. It is also popular for bonsai cultivation. One of the oldest specimen zelkovas in Japan, known as the giant keyaki of Noma, lives at Noma Shrine in Nose-cho, a town near Osaka. It is believed to be more than 1,000 years of age and is protected as a state-designated natural monument.

ZELKOVA SERRATA

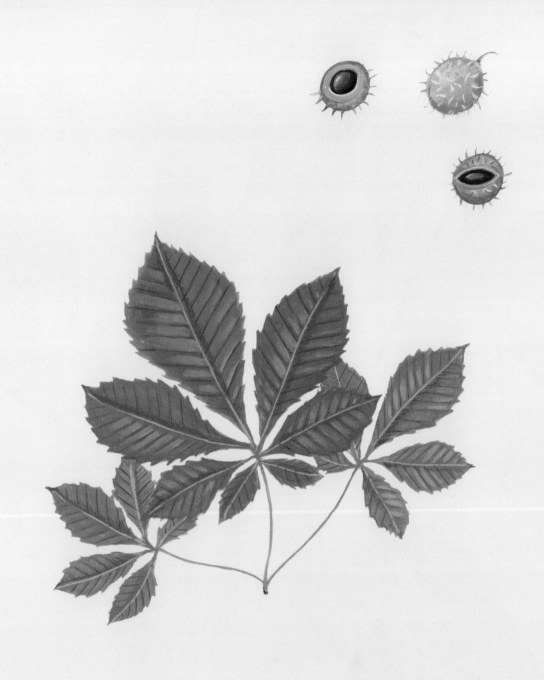

GLOSSARY

aerial root	specialised rooting structures arising from the above-ground stem.
anther	the terminal part of a stamen that contains the pollen.
apetalous	flower that does not bear petals.
aril	an extra seed covering typically coloured and hairy or fleshy.
(leaf) axil	the upper angle between the leaf stalk and the stem or branch.
bipinnate	a compound leaf arrangement with leaflets in opposite pairs.
calyx	part of a flower that encloses the petals with a protective layer when in bud.
CITES	Convention on International Trade in Endangered Species of Wild Fauna and Flora.
clonal colony	group of genetically identical organisms, produced asexually from one stock.
compound (leaf)	consisting of several or many distinct leaflets joined to a single stem.
conifer	cone-bearing woody plant, generally a tree.
corymb	a flower cluster where the flowers form a flat or slightly convex head.
cultivar	a plant variety developed in cultivation through selective breeding.
drupe/drupelet	a thin-skinned fleshy fruit with a central stone containing a seed, e.g. cherry.
Dutch elm disease	a serious disease that affects elm trees and is caused by a fungus.
elliptical	possessing an oval shape.
endemic	a plant that is native or restricted to a certain locality.
entire (margin)	having a smooth, non-serrated profile.
epiphyte	a plant that grows on another plant, especially one that is not parasitic.
fastigiated	having branches more or less parallel to the main stem.
follicle	a dry fruit, opening on one side to release its seeds.
genus	a classification that ranks above species and below family.
hesperidium	a fruit with sectioned pulp inside a separable rind, e.g. an orange.

indigenous	originating or occurring naturally in a particular place.
IUCN Red List	the International Union for Conservation of Nature list of threatened species.
inflorescence	the complete floral parts of a plant.
laurophyllic	relating to broadleaved evergreen plants of ancient evolutionary origin.
masting	seed production synchronised with that of other plants of the same species.
monocotyledon	a flowering plant with an embryo that bears a single seed leaf or cotyledon.
mutation	the altered structure of genes or chromosomes, resulting in a variant form.
naturalise	to establish a plant to live wild in a region where it is not indigenous.
operculum	a specialised botanical structure that acts as a cap, flap or lid.
ovate	having an oval outline, like an egg.
pampas	an area of South America characterised by extensive treeless plains.
palmate	a leaf with five or more lobes whose midribs all radiate from one point.
panicle	a loosely branching cluster of flowers.
pinnate	leaflets arranged on either side of the leaf stem, typically in opposite pairs.
pollination	the transfer of pollen to a stigma, ovule, flower, or plant allowing fertilisation.
raceme	a cluster of flowers attached by short equal stalks along a central stem.
receptacle	the thickened part of a stem from which the floral parts arise.
samara	a winged hard fruit, e.g. nut, containing one seed, as in ash or maple.
semi-evergreen	retaining persistent functional foliage during part of the year or dry season.
sepal	outer part of a flower enclosing the petals, typically green and leaf-like.
stamen	the male reproductive part of a flower consisting of anther and filament.
style	the part of a female flower that connects between the pistil and the ovary.
synonym	a word or phrase with similar meaning to another word or phrase.

taxonomy	the branch of science concerned with classification, e.g. of organisms.
tepal	part of the outer whorl of a flower undifferentiated between petal or sepal.
truncheoning	the cutting and planting of part of a plant as a means of propagation.

INDEX

Michael Jordan is an Honours Graduate in Botany, University of London, his writing career began after ten years as a successful broadcaster working for BBC TV, Granada, Anglia, Channel 4, Radio 4 and World Service. He has published ten books on the natural world, his most recent being *The Beauty of Trees*. He lives in Devon.

Kelly Louise Judd received a BFA from the Kansas City Art Institute and continues to live in Kansas City, MO. She has exhibited her flora, fauna, and folklore inspired artwork in New Orleans, LA, Nashville, TN and throughout the United States. Her illustrations have been featured in children's books, magazines, and on natural product labels. When she is not working on her art she can often be found outdoors tending one of her gardens or simply staring at plants.

Brimming with creative inspiration, how-to projects and useful information to enrich your everyday life, Quarto Knows is a favourite destination for those pursuing their interests and passions. Visit our site and dig deeper with our books into your area of interest: Quarto Creates, Quarto Cooks, Quarto Homes, Quarto Lives, Quarto Drives, Quarto Explores, Quarto Gifts, or Quarto Kids.

First published in 2018 by White Lion Publishing
an imprint of The Quarto Group
The Old Brewery, 6 Blundell Street
London N7 9BH
United Kingdom

www.QuartoKnows.com

A catalogue record for this book is available from the British Library.

ISBN 978 1 78131 741 9
Ebook ISBN 978 1 78131 848 5

10 9 8 7 6 5 4 3 2 1
2022 2021 2020 2019 2018

Illustrations by Kelly Louise Judd

Printed in China